"**Living with Loss** is a fountain of hope
they will get through another day after
filled with daily gems of inspiration, advice, and common sense."
—Dr. Gloria Horsley, President and Founder of Open to Hope

Living
with
Loss,
One Day
at a Time

Rachel Blythe Kodanaz

Living
with
Loss,

*One Day
at a Time*

Living
with
Loss,
One Day
at a Time

Rachel Blythe Kodanaz

FULCRUM
GOLDEN, COLORADO

Library of Congress Cataloging-in-Publication Data on file

Printed in the United States of America
0 9 8 7 6 5 4 3 2 1

Design by Jack Lenzo

Fulcrum Publishing
4690 Table Mountain Dr., Ste. 100
Golden, CO 80403
800-992-2908 • 303-277-1623
www.fulcrumbooks.com

For Rod.
You taught me how to love and to live.

For those who trusted me over the years
with their personal stories.

Contents

Foreword

When my dad passed away without warning, I embodied the meaning of grief-stricken. My mom was in the late stages of Alzheimer's disease, and my dad was her caretaker. I was totally blindsided because I was just coming to terms with my mom's illness, and my dad's mortality had not been in question. I was shocked to find myself so distraught by my dad's death—nothing had ever taken my breath away like sudden and total grief. In one powerless instant, I had to face the realities that I would never see my dad again and that nothing in life is permanent. I was unprepared to enter this new world and convinced that the unbearable pain would last forever.

Professionally, I was in the middle of a fast-paced production schedule in Chicago, shooting my second season of a successful television documentary series. For the first time in my life, I was devoid of motivation and purpose. Ten days after my dad's funeral, I flew to Chicago for a five-day shoot. While getting ready for day one of filming, I collapsed on my hotel room floor. The crew was waiting for me and I couldn't move. I didn't want to move. Like a prisoner shackled by pain, I gave myself permission to make one phone call. It took all the strength

I had to find Rachel's number in my phone and hit send. She was my go-to person, and not just because I knew she was an expert in this area—after all, I did have a front-row seat when her husband literally dropped dead, leaving her with their two-year-old. I also called Rachel because I had an indelible image of her *no longer grieving*. I will never forget being witness to Rachel's embrace of grief. I watched, listened, and learned as she steadily harnessed the power of grief. Grief propelled her to take inventory of her life goals, to compete in the Ironman in Hawaii, and ultimately to help others live with loss. In my darkest hour, Rachel's magical journey gave me hope.

Rachel answered before I had a chance to give up on the idea of reaching out to her. At first she just listened as I cried. She then reminded me that I would not feel this way forever. She knew that was one of my biggest fears. She also knew I needed to get out of my room. She suggested something really simple to me. Rachel asked me if the crew knew I had just lost my dad. I told her they didn't. She gently pointed out that I could tell them. It was such a simple concept, but I was not thinking little thoughts, I was focusing on big questions that had no answers, like, "Why do people die when they do?" Rachel was also subtly suggesting that I didn't have to grieve in silence. Grief is a very personal experience, yet we don't have to feel alone. Something shifted for me that day when I shared my story with the crew at lunch. I was empowered at a time when I felt out of control, and I felt connected at a time when I was so detached. My journey through grief was long and hard, but Rachel helped me put one foot in front of the other—which was all I needed to get there.

I am so glad that Rachel wrote this book, so she can continue to help more people live with loss. She has a special gift for imparting small and manageable ideas that can profoundly impact someone grieving. Loss is never easy, but Rachel's words and wisdom can help make the journey a bit more bearable and perhaps even more meaningful.

Sharon Liese

Executive Producer—Herizon Productions

Acknowledgments

To Gretchen, for holding my hand while we embraced our journey together.

To Taner, for loving us unconditionally.

To those who stood by my side, lifted me up, and proved there was more life to live, I will forever be thankful.

Introduction

It was a perfect life; one that many would be envious of. One that I always dreamed of but thought only occurred in the movies—mainly because my life until then was nothing like the movies. There were many life hardships that got me to where I was, but despite my hurt and self-doubt, I found the perfect husband, gave birth to a wonderful daughter, maintained a fulfilling career, and lived in a house full of love, laughter, and happiness. Just when Rod had helped me to build the life of my dreams, April 14, 1992, arrived and my world ended. I spoke to my husband at 5:20 PM and told him I would pick up our daughter, Gretchen, from day care and would meet him at home. I got home, and he wasn't there, nor would he ever return. He passed away leaving his office at the age of thirty-two.

My first reaction was that my perfect life had come to an end. How could this happen? Why me? Haven't I been through enough? Bad things aren't supposed to happen to good people. It took me many years of tears and sleepless nights to realize my perfect life did not end—it changed. And while change is not what I wanted, it has taught me how to appreciate and find joy in the little things. I cannot deny how devastated I was by Rod's death, nor can I deny how long it took me to smile and laugh again. The important thing is I can.

By profession, I am a logical person. Therefore, I need to understand everything—I don't need to master everything, just understand. As my family teases, I am only black and white—no gray. With Rod's death my logic was lost. My emotions took over, and I couldn't help but waffle in my decisions, hide, run, and cry. While it proves to be the answer for some, turning to religion for help wasn't an option. I've never been a very religious person and had trouble adding my logic to religion. I read almost every book on grief but was often aggravated, as they were either written more from a spiritual point of view, or they did not offer suggestions or ideas for helping me to cope with my new situation. Here I was, a single mother of a toddler and working full time. It took all my energy and strength to get through bath time and still be a happy, supportive, and loving mother for my daughter.

As I went down the path of the unknown with Gretchen, I searched for answers to my questions, stability in my life, happiness in my heart, and a smile for my face. I learned so much, I ignored so much, and I hurt so much. My journey brought me to support others on their journey of grief. Beginning in the workplace, I began helping coworkers and managers understand the needs and support that grieving employees would want when they returned to work or when a coworker passed. I shared hope with other fellow grievers by presenting on a variety of important topics and facilitating support groups in an effort to help them find their path, all the while finding my place in my new life, absorbing the conversations and integrating them into my life and my journey. Time allowed me to once again find my love, create a new family, and live in a house full of love, laughter, and happiness.

My outlook on grief and loss, my supporters, and my life experiences provided me with insight on how to endure one day at a time the setbacks we encounter with grief.

This book doesn't make assumptions about readers' background, beliefs, or prior experiences. Instead, it presents a full range of practical insights and suggestions. The main goal of this book is to provide a down-to-earth, commonsensical approach to living with loss. To this end, the book is filled with unedited personal experiences and working examples of all topics covered. It is not intended to be a complete, single source of inspiration but rather a simple and straightforward reference guide to pick up and use whenever you feel the need. If you choose, you can read the book in one sitting, or just a portion at a time—there is no start or end, just your own personal journey.

Day 1

Beginning the Journey

You have lost a loved one, and your grief journey is just beginning. The funeral is over, those around you have resumed their daily lives, and your new life without your loved one has just begun.

Where do you begin the journey? With you!

Start with the essentials of life—taking care of yourself and your health. The better you feel, the better you will operate. Make it a priority to eat well, sleep regularly, exercise often, and let those who love you care for you. Accepting a helping hand will allow you to take care of yourself. Embrace food others have brought over; allow someone to empty your dishwasher or bathe your children.

At times you may not have the desire to eat—so find something to nibble on. Take a walk around the block or at least walk out the door for some fresh air.

Today, it is about *you*.

Day 4
Unspeakable Grief

A few years ago, I attended the funeral of an eighteen-year-old who had been attending his freshman year of college. As I listened to his father share a eulogy with hundreds of attendees, he used a phrase that I will never forget: "unspeakable grief."

I listened to his words while watching the sadness in his face as he shared his story at the podium that cold winter morning. He taught me a great lesson of the meaning of unspeakable grief. One cannot speak when there are no words to truly articulate the feeling of overwhelming sadness, the inability to comprehend the loss, and the continual search each day for the will to carry on.

We will survive, and while we may not be able to speak in words, we are speaking—in love, loss, and the desire to remember.

Day 5
You Held Their Hand

As we search for answers following the death of a loved one, we often wish the end were different.

For those who experienced a sudden death, we are torn between not having been able to say good-bye and being thankful that our loved one did not suffer. For those who experienced a slower death, we are thankful for the days and weeks during which we were able to share emotional thoughts.

Whether your loss was a sudden death or a long illness, you held your loved one's hands for the last time and said good-bye. May the love you shared triumph over the pain and bring you comfort for time you had together.

Day 6
Two Tiers of Grievers

Why, after a loss, do we connect with some friends or family members and not others? A simple explanation—there are two tiers of grievers:

- First-tier grievers are those who are grieving the loss of someone special.
- Second-tier grievers are those who are grieving for the griever.

When I lost my husband, I found a direct connection to his family, as we were all first-tier grievers—grieving the loss of their son and brother and my husband. I considered my sisters to be second-tier grievers; even though they lost their brother-in-law, their grief was directed toward me.

This is a concept I discovered years into my grief journey, and in hindsight it was helpful to know why I clung to some people and not others. Bottom line—I emotionally related to them.

Day 7
Tell Your Story

Everyone has a story, but yours is unique to you. Embrace it and share it!

Tell it a thousand times.

As you share, listen to yourself as you speak:

- Embrace the love.
- Embrace the loss.
- Embrace the sadness.
- Smile.
- Cry.
- Feel all the emotions.
- Share the story with pictures.

Keep telling your story—people will keep listening!

Day 8

Don't Worry, as They Already Knew

Regret is often a common form of sorrow after we lose a loved one. If only we had told our loved ones what we were thinking or what was troubling us. We can spend days, months, and years wishing we had one more chance to share our thoughts. Instead, we can just know in our hearts that they already knew what we were thinking.

Regret is an emotional reaction to past acts and behaviors—usually linked to sadness, embarrassment, or guilt. You cannot change the past after the death of a loved one, so do not feel remorse, but instead, look forward.

To help you move from regret to "we lived our lives to the fullest," remember that your loved one knew you better than you could have imagined, and they knew you loved them.

Day 13

Is What I Am Feeling Normal?

While grief is a natural and normal response to a loss, the journey will vary based on the individuals and their circumstances. Grief can feel intense and complex. We will all experience grief at some point in our lives and might experience similar phases or stages, but the timeline will differ based on the person who has passed away, our relationship with the person, the type of death, family ties, and our individual coping mechanisms.

So, what is normal? Everything you are feeling is normal, as it is your reaction to the loss. Most grievers will experience several aspects of grief:

- Numbness
- Shock
- Denial
- Anger
- Guilt

- Disorientation
- Depression
- Panic
- Acceptance

Please remember, though, that these feelings don't occur in the same way or in the same order for any two people. Your response is based on your unique circumstances of the loss of a loved one. You are not going crazy—your reaction is normal!

Day 14

A Soothing Cup of Tea

What is it about a cup of tea that can soothe you when you are sick, relax you after a hard day at work, and warm you on a cold winter's day? The combination of tea leaves and hot water creates a cup of rest and relaxation.

Specifically, tea leaves contain seven hundred chemicals, including amino acids that reduce mental and physical stress. In addition, consumption of tea is known to calm you, while allowing you to remain focused and alert.

Whether you prefer herbal, black, or green tea, enjoy a cup of warmth to help you get through today.

Day 15
Do One Thing at a Time

Experiencing grief often takes the logic out of our daily thoughts. We often try to do too much, resulting in disappointment and discouragement. One "logical" solution: to avoid being overwhelmed, try not to multitask.

Create a list of what you need to accomplish, getting it out of your mind and onto paper. This will allow you to clear your thoughts. Prioritize the list, decide what is important, delegate if possible, and work your way down the list, feeling good about your accomplishments. Finish one task at a time, focusing on completion and accuracy.

Rome was not built in a day, nor does your list need to be accomplished in one. Simply do the best you can.

Day 16
Clichés of Grief

Some of us experience hurtful comments from friends and family as they search for ways to help ease our pain. The remarks are usually said with the best of intentions but are misunderstood by the griever as insensitive.

Cliché	Initial Reaction	What They Meant
Time will heal.	Do we really ever heal, or does time soften the pain?	You must feel as though the pain will never end.
You are young, you can have more children.	Even if I do, a new child will not replace the one I lost.	You must really be sad; let me hug you again.
Call me if I can help.	Most likely I won't.	I would like to come by tomorrow and . . .
He is in a better place.	No, he isn't. The better place is sitting next to me.	It isn't fair, is it?
You are holding up so well.	Right? Maybe on the outside.	I am available to visit with you. Can I call you tomorrow?
It is time to move on!	Move on from what?	Take the time you need, I just miss your smile.

People are not mean spirited; they just don't know what to say. As a griever, please try to filter out the "hurtful" gestures and interpret them as love and caring.

Day 17

Pictures of Your Loved One

Why is it that some grievers can look at pictures of their loved ones and find warmth, while others need to place them face down on the table to avoid looking at them? For certain grievers, the pain of seeing a picture is too heartbreaking, while others receive comfort by looking at and sharing photos as if their loved one is still alive.

Immediately following a sudden death, looking at pictures can create anger and other negative emotions. Often I am asked, "When does this change, and instead of sadness, I will cherish the photos?" Usually, once the shock has worn off and you begin to digest that the loss really has occurred, you find comfort in gazing into the eyes of your loved one.

Day 18

Find Your Comfort Food

We all have comfort foods that make us feel better. There is something about a chocolate candy bar that makes us feel relaxed or an ice-cream cone that makes us feel refreshed.

There are so many categories of comfort food. For some, eating right provides comfort, as the griever is less lethargic. For others, reaching into the cookie jar will console their emotions. Some feel having a full stomach will help them fall asleep. Anything in moderation will be helpful for the immediate "high" the food has to offer. As your journey proceeds, your comfort foods will change along the way.

What is your comfort food?

Day 19
Schedule a Realistic Day

What was once realistic to accomplish in one day may have changed for you since your loss. Before you plan your day, think about what really needs to be accomplished.

First, tackle the have-tos—those tasks that must be done, including taking care of yourself, your children, and your parents, as well as going to work, light housekeeping, and family commitments. Once you have successfully completed those tasks, attempt your prioritized list of responsibilities. Only attempt the items you can juggle with your day, including returning a phone call, going to the grocery store, reading the unopened mail, or sending a thank-you note.

Each day as you feel stronger, add additional tasks to your list. Be sure to pace yourself, as feeling overwhelmed only increases your anxiety.

Day 20

Back to Normal

Following the funeral, people around you often expect you to resume life as it was before the loss. Their expectation is that you will be back to normal and exist as if nothing has happened.

But for many of you, following the funeral means you now need to clean out your parent's home, distributing the belongings to siblings and family members, followed by selling the property. For those of you who have lost a spouse, you will have to complete paperwork, organize personal belongings, and determine financial needs, while caring for your children.

The funeral is only the first step after the loss—then comes adjusting to your new life, which has changed forever.

While you find your "new normal" and resume your new life, let others around you adapt to that normal.

Day 21
Minor Decisions

Every grief book I have ever read suggests not making any major decisions in the early days of grief. This mainly refers to selling a house, quitting a job, moving to a different state, or cleaning out the closets. The advice makes sense, as your journey is just beginning, and your emotions and outlook on life will change during the course of your recovery.

Do go ahead and make the minor decisions that are important to you and your family. Often following a loss, we flounder and are overwhelmed when making decisions—even if they are small—such as taking time off from work, going on a vacation, meeting a friend for a cocktail, painting the house, or buying a much-needed new car.

Try not to question yourself about whether the decision is good or bad, right or wrong—just decide!

Day 22
Ask for Help

Why is it so difficult for us to ask for help? Possibly because it prolongs the realization of admitting that we cannot do everything while we are grieving.

The truth is, people around you want to help so desperately. They would do anything to lessen the pain in your heart and the stress the loss has created. They ask you to call if you need anything, but you are reluctant to call. Most likely when you are really in need of support, you will reach out to the handful of people who are a part of your daily activities or a close family member.

I would gently suggest that you try keeping a list of tasks you could use some assistance with, and next time your friends call and ask what they can do for you, look at your list and ask for help.

Day 23
Lend a Hand

Advice to those who want to help: don't ask—just do it. In other words, if you ask the griever what you can do to help, the answer will be "nothing." Look around the griever's house; there is plenty you can do. A few ideas include:

- Help with carpooling.
- Drop off dinner at the griever's house.
- Run some errands.
- Mow the lawn.
- Fix the leaky sink.
- Empty the dishwasher.
- Plant some flowers for spring.
- Shovel the driveway.
- Visit often.
- Be present.

Think of what you need. Grievers need the same things.

Day 24

Reentry after the Loss

Most people who are grieving a significant loss have a tendency to spend time at home away from daily activities, including school and work. The feeling of not being ready to be social, not wanting to explain what has happened with their loved one, or not feeling like explaining how they are doing is overwhelming. At some point, you will want to come out of your bubble, and you will find the desire to reenter into a customary schedule. Here are a few suggestions for taking it slow:

- Start with short days at school or work.
- Keep your schedule to a minimum.
- Realize you are a different person from who you were before the loss.
- Remember to eat, sleep, and exercise.
- If you look good, you will feel good. Dress like you care.
- Surround yourself with upbeat people.
- Talk about your loved one, as avoiding the topic creates stress.

Day 25

Grief Is Unpredictable

Be aware that grief is unpredictable. You may feel extreme highs and extreme lows during your journey. Some days you will feel content, with no desire to cry, and other days you will find yourself very irrational in all aspects of your life. Trying to predict if you will have a good day or a bad day is like looking into a crystal ball.

Take each day as it comes, and know that one day will be good and on another you might take a step backward. Embrace the setback, and work on getting back on your feet.

Day 26
Give Yourself Some TLC

Today is for you—give yourself some tender loving care. Leave your cell phone at home, turn off your computer, and leave the dishes in the sink.

- Go get your hair cut—let someone wash your hair and massage your scalp.
- Play a round of golf without worrying about what you should be doing.
- Get a manicure and pedicure, and be sure to choose a happy color.
- Buy a new outfit; feel good about yourself.
- Have a special lunch with some friends or family.
- Indulge in foods you usually avoid.
- Get a massage.
- Hire a babysitter and let her put your kids to bed.
- Go for a walk around the neighborhood after dinner.
- Curl up and read a book.

Or whatever else you can think of for *you*!

Day 27

Is One Loss More Significant Than Another?

The most significant loss is yours. If your loss is your spouse, there is no greater loss than being widowed. If your loss is a child, there is no greater loss than the death of a child. If your loss is a parent, there is no greater loss than saying good-bye to a parent. If your loss is your pet, there is no greater loss for you.

When a loss occurs, it is natural to want to connect with others who have experienced a similar loss. A widow will connect with a widow, and a parent who lost a child will connect with another parent in a similar situation. When different types of losses intersect, it is human nature to compare them—parents will share that there is nothing worse than losing a child, but would they really know what it is like to be widowed and climbing into an empty bed?

Be cautious of comparing your loss with others. Instead, provide support and understanding to your fellow grievers, and be tolerant of the fact that their loss to them is just as significant as yours is to you.

Day 28
It Takes a Village

No doubt those who are grieving must walk their own grief journey, and the process might feel like one of isolation. Actually, you are not alone. The journey *is* personal; however, your community is ready to provide support and care as needed.

Your village includes family, friends, religious affiliations, counselors, support groups, teachers, coworkers, and neighbors.

Embrace your special community!

Day 29
Crying

Crying soothes our minds, makes us feel better, and reduces our stress.

Let it out, and wipe your tears.

Day 30
Self-Doubt

Why is it that grief is so powerful that it knocks you off your feet? Even once secure, reliable, and confident people can become skeptical of all aspects of their lives while they are grieving.

Emotions associated with grief and loss are often so overwhelming that your reaction is to doubt your decisions, relationships, and abilities. In your heart of hearts, you know you are doing the best you can, but you have uncertainty regarding your surroundings.

When friends do not call—you think they have moved on, don't care, or that you have offended them with your tears.

When your children act up—you question your parenting skills rather than thinking they are simply being children.

When your family struggles with your parent's estate—you take it personally, as if you were the one causing the conflict.

Self-doubt will go away as fast as it showed up. Be patient with yourself, and you will regain your confidence.

Day 31

Journaling

Why should you journal?

Journaling provides an outlet for you to be alone with your thoughts and emotions, allowing you to express yourself and your feelings in writing. By revisiting earlier days of writing, journaling on a daily or weekly basis will allow you to measure your progress in working through your grief.

A journal can be very personal, allowing you privacy to reflect while capturing good and bad thoughts you may not feel comfortable sharing with others. The physical form of a journal can be a notebook, Day-Timer, or electronic file. To help you get started, here are some thought triggers for daily entries:

- Dear . . . (Who are you writing to? Yourself, the deceased, a child, and so forth)
- Today I . . .
- I was really angry with . . .
- I did it! For the first time . . .
- I am afraid of . . .
- Tomorrow, I will try to . . .
- The kids hit a milestone today, they . . .
- After my counselor appointment today, I . . .
- I know the days are getting better because . . .

- I don't think I can make it anymore. Today was especially hard because . . .
- It is amazing what a new day can bring . . .
- Getting up and dressed this morning, I . . .

Start journaling today!

Day 32
Honor Your Loved One Today

Start your day today with honoring your loved ones in a special way.

Make their favorite meal, wear a piece of jewelry or clothing they gave you, bake their favorite dessert, walk in their favorite park, flip through photos of your favorite trip with them, or call one of their closest friends. Reconnect with your loved ones by honoring them with wonderful memories you shared together.

Day 33

Take a Bath

Fill your tub to the brim with warm water, add soap containing the perfect blend of relaxing fragrances, and climb in.

Close your eyes, smell the scents, and relax!

Sounds fabulous, doesn't it? The bath will feel as good as it sounds.

Day 34
Why Am I Doing Stupid Things?

Because there is no logic with grief—only emotions. You are walking around in the fog we spoke of earlier. I will share a story with you in hope that you will find humor in some of the "stupid" things you are doing.

I went from a two-income family to single mom when my husband passed away. I panicked about money, which resulted in a decision to discontinue the support I was receiving from the person who helped clean my house and the boy who cut my lawn. Instead, on the weekends when I was exhausted from working all week, I hired a babysitter to watch my child while I cut the grass and cleaned my house. I can laugh now, since I used the money I was paying the cleaner and mower to pay the babysitter. There was no logic—just trying to save money—but in the end, I was spending less time with my daughter and not saving any money.

As a griever, the tendency is to respond to the current situation without looking into the future, which often results in making stupid decisions. Laugh at these stupid decisions.

Day 35

Sleeping Patterns

How can you walk around so tired, yet you cannot get a full night's sleep?

Falling asleep is not usually the challenge for grievers; in fact, you often walk around in a zombie state, wishing you could climb into bed. Instead, staying asleep is usually the challenge—the four-o'clock-in-the-morning internal alarm clock seems to wake up most grievers. Try not to be discouraged about sleeping, as this phase will pass eventually. Meanwhile, here are a few suggestions to help:

- Eat a good dinner.
- Take it easy on the dessert.
- Drink alcohol in moderation.

Relax before bedtime—take a bath, read a book, or watch television.

Day 36
Personal Belongings

No need to rush into determining what is best for your loved one's personal belongings.

For today, savor the meaning of each belonging. If possible, wear your loved one's clothing or jewelry, bring his stuffed animal with you in your car, or drink from her favorite mug. Remember the loved one with each item and take pleasure in the moment.

Future daily entries will suggest building memorials, distributing the possessions to the appropriate person, or ways to save what is important to you.

Day 37

Dedications at Special Events

Ask ten different grieving family members how they feel about mentioning your loved one at a special event, and you will receive ten different suggestions. Here is mine:

You are who you are in life, partially because of who has entered and exited your life as you have grown. Dedications to a significant loved one at a graduation, wedding, baptism, Bar/Bat Mitzvah, or anniversary party will allow you to keep the relationship central to your life. A toast, comment, picture, or gesture is appropriate, as long as you do not make it the focal point, detracting from the special event.

Day 38
Finding Grief Support

When mourning the loss of someone special, we often find the need to step outside the circle of our immediate family and friends for support. Spending time with people who are walking a similar path can provide insight and assistance in a different way from those who are close to us.

Support groups can be found in your area by contacting hospitals, hospices, or religious associations. Additional support is available on the Internet through personal blogs and online chat rooms. Look for a group where you find a connection to the people attending as well as to the program. Whether the group meets in person or online, talking to others will provide encouragement and assistance.

Day 39

Honoring Your Loved One through Special Rituals

Rituals take on a different meaning after the loss of someone special. Cooking the loved one's favorite meal, setting the table in a certain manner, and having family sit in assigned seats can be considered a ritual.

The goal is to honor and memorialize your loved one by doing something special as a tribute to the person and as an expression of gratitude or praise. Some people choose to perform rituals on special occasions, whereas others do so at their own discretion.

Whether you choose to honor your loved one through a morning ritual, a prayer at mealtime, a special song before running a road race, or as part of a holiday celebration, consider the gesture a special way of spending time together.

Day 40

Do We Really Ever Say Good-Bye?

As you walk through your journey of grief, saying good-bye will occur in stages.

- At the hospital, hospice, or morgue, you physically say good-bye.
- At the funeral or celebration ceremony, you say good-bye with friends and family.
- When you bury the casket or distribute the ashes, you say good-bye with a ritual.
- When you clean out the closet, you say good-bye to the belongings.
- As time goes by without your loved one, you say good-bye to creating new memories.
- As you take new photos, you say good-bye to including your loved one in the pictures.

Wishing farewell to your loved ones occurs in stages and lasts forever—as we really never say a final good-bye—they are a part of who you are and who you will become. Savor the stages.

Day 41

Is There a Right Way to Grieve?

This is your journey, your schedule, and your time to mourn the loss of someone very close. While there are simple suggestions to help lessen the sadness along the way, how you proceed is up to you. No two people grieve the same, and there is no reason for anyone to criticize what is best for you. While others will make suggestions about what you should be doing, in the end it is up to you to determine what is best for you. No two people grieve the same, so it will be difficult for others to tell you what is right for you.

There is no right or wrong way; the path you have chosen is right for you.

Day 42

Make "Me" Time Every Day

What are you doing for *you* today?

- Take a walk.
- Partake in yoga.
- Bake a treat—then eat it with a cup of tea or glass of milk.
- Read a book.
- Work out at the gym.
- Get a manicure and pedicure.
- Plant flowers.
- Call a friend.
- Download your favorite music.
- Watch a favorite TV show.
- Lie in the sun.
- Meditate.
- Take a deep breath.
- Walk on the beach.

Start thinking about what you will do for *you* tomorrow.

Day 43

Relax Your Standards for Nonessentials

What tasks really need to be accomplished today?

There are tasks that we must do as part of the essentials of life—eat, sleep, work, care for children, and go to work. Then there are other tasks that make us feel good after we accomplish them, but the price tag attached means we often compromise on the essentials—mainly sleep.

For some, not being able to "get it all done" creates additional stress, resulting in letdowns that complicate your grief journey. By relaxing the standards you created before the loss, you will not be as disappointed when you find it difficult to accomplish everything you think you should. Leaving dishes in the sink overnight is okay, not reading the daily newspaper and placing it directly into the recycle bin is okay, stopping at the grocery store for precooked food is okay, and skipping a night of reading a book to your child is okay.

Figure out what can put off by relaxing your preloss standards and determining what is essential and what can wait for another day.

Day 44
Coping with Change

Change is often difficult regardless of the cause. With the recent loss of someone special, your life has changed in many ways. The impact of the change will depend on the interaction you had with the person you lost.

The changes in your life occur whether you want them to or not, so do your best to embrace them by taking one day at a time. Try not to look at your future; instead, aim only to look at today. Know your limits; try not to exceed what you are physically or emotionally capable of doing in one day. Develop a positive attitude, even though some days it may be difficult.

Bottom line—change is the process of becoming different, so be aware of the shifts as your life is changing.

Day 45

Why Am I So Exhausted?

Grieving is exhausting.

Often excessive fatigue is in direct correlation to emotional imbalance. Even if you are sleeping ten hours a night and napping in the afternoon, you are probably still extremely worn out.

All your emotional energy is being consumed by your grief. What you are feeling is normal. Continue to eat well and sleep when you can, and in time your emotions will find balance with your physical needs, providing you with more energy. Hang in there!

Day 46

What You Should and Shouldn't Do

Why is it that when you are grieving, everyone around you is the expert on grief—even though they have not experienced a loss such as yours? They tell you *what* you should and shouldn't do. In fact, they even tell you *how* you should or shouldn't do something.

What makes them the experts? Actually, they are not experts, nor do they really want to be experts in loss. The truth is that in their hearts they are searching for a way to help you with your loss and grief. They desperately want to make you feel better and lessen your sorrow. In essence, they want to fix you.

What you should do is:

- Take care of yourself.
- Connect with others you can relate to.
- Have patience with yourself.
- Have tolerance for others who are trying to help.
- Continue to talk about your loved one.

What you shouldn't do is:

- Compromise your beliefs.
- Take advice from others if you do not feel comfortable with their approach.
- Rush into making decisions.
- Place judgment on those who are trying to help.

Day 47

Let People Know What You Need

Everyone needs different forms of support when they are mourning the loss of someone they love. Some need to be alone, while others want people around them continuously. Some need to cry, while others need to be somber. Some need to keep busy, while others want to sit and reflect. Some find comfort in food, while others have no desire to eat. Some like to exercise, while others would rather sit on a couch.

Let the people around you know what is best for you and your family. Communicate your needs, whether you need reinforcement of love and support, help with dinners, an ear to listen to you about your loved one, space to be alone, or frequent invitations for dinner or an outing. Your desires will change as time goes on—try to keep the lines of communication open, so others will be there to support you.

Day 48
Anger

Anger is an emotional response related to the feeling of being offended, wronged, or violated. Being angry is a natural reaction following the loss of a loved one. When my husband passed away, I remember throwing his toothbrush across the room and yelling at him for doing this to me. Of course, he did nothing to me, but the anger at the loss made me react by lashing out at him.

Anger has good and bad aspects during your journey. On the positive side, anger creates a vehicle to release negative emotions and provides a platform to manage extreme emotions. Sometimes being angry might allow you to settle down when you are extremely distraught over something specific. The negative side of anger is the negative health impact. Often anger increases blood pressure, heart rate, and adrenaline flow, causing a headache, feeling of being nauseous, or muscle tension. In moderation, this is acceptable, but prolonged anger is not a healthy way to work through your grief.

Try to determine its sources to help resolve your rage. While anger is a normal response to grief, there is usually a specific trigger on any given day that causes a reaction. Find a positive way to work through your anger: talk to someone, go for a walk, play the piano, take a bath, or write your thoughts on paper.

Day 49

Individual Grief Journey

Each morning as you wake up you embark on yet another day of your journey. No two days seem to be identical, and just when you think you are beginning to grasp the concept, something triggers a slight setback. You wake up the next day and start all over again.

Spending time with grievers over the years, I have heard them describe their journey as the feeling that they were drowning and not able to climb out of the water, or suffocating as if someone had a pillow over their face. Grief has the ability to literally suck the wind out of our lungs. The overpowering feeling is part of the journey—the physical and emotional pieces merging together with great force. We all know we will have the ability to catch our next breath, but we don't know if we will be able to survive the overwhelming feeling of pain associated with the grief.

Somehow, though, the force finds its way to neutralize itself, and we can breathe again. While each new day may feel as bad as the day before, it's not. Continue your individual journey with hope.

Day 50
Saying No

Having the ability to say no to someone is a gift. The majority of people do not have the ability to say no to a social invitation, so they find themselves dancing around the invitation with a variety of excuses, making it very uncomfortable for both parties. What you really want to do is say no to the invitation, possibly because you are not ready to socialize yet. Unfortunately, the next round of questions and concerns arise from the person offering the invitation. "Why don't you want to go?," "You should get out more," "We would love for you to join us," "There will be other single people there," and a variety of other comments.

One suggestion for handling the invitations is to say no for today, while encouraging the hosts to ask again. Simply suggest this particular outing will not work for you, but that you would like them to keep you in mind for the future. This allows you the chance to let time go by, as you may change your mind about or outlook for being social. Who knows what the future will bring?

Day 51
Healing Trinkets

As children, we often held an object in our hand as we lay in bed or were being pushed in a stroller—a form of security and familiarity. A healing trinket is just that: an object that provides us with strength and warmth, reminding us of our loved one.

A healing trinket can be an angel representing a spirit or messenger or a picture of your loved one. Some carry rosary beads, while others carry a teddy bear. My healing trinket was a wooden heart I carried in my purse for years, knowing the love of my husband would be carried with me wherever I went.

What is yours?

Day 52
Who Is Your Angel?

This is the special person who is looking over your shoulder during these difficult days. The caring, loving person with whom you can share whatever is on your mind—and he or she won't think you are about to jump off a bridge. This individual will not judge your decisions, tell you how you should feel, or tell you it is time to get over the loss.

You may have multiple angels in your life fulfilling different needs and comforting you in a variety of ways. The individual is always present in your life and saying the right things at the right time—the things you really need to hear.

Your angel may be a family member, friend, coworker, distant relative, neighbor, or God—a guiding light helping you find your way through your special grief journey.

If you don't have an angel, find one! If you do, embrace and trust this person, as he or she will guide you.

Day 53
The Red Flag

The red flag is a symbol of protest—or in this case, not having the strength to accept your situation and not being able to cope. Dealing with the loss of a loved one is likely to be the most difficult event in your life. Therefore, if you find yourself exercising self-destructive behavior, partaking in substance abuse, engaging in workplace failures, or burning social bridges, it is time to find support with an individual professional or support group.

The behavior is a normal reaction to your situation; however, it is detrimental to working through grief. In most cases, the behaviors will prolong your journey and interfere with finding relief from your pain.

Please, reach out for help and trust the person or group providing the support.

Day 54
Smile

A smile can make all the difference in the world to your mood. Whether it is you who is smiling or someone who is smiling at you, the energy is warm and inviting.

A smile is a facial expression showing happiness, joy, or pleasure about something or someone. Even in our darkest place, we have plenty we can smile about. A smile is a great way of conveying thoughts and feelings, and most important, a smile is contagious. You smile and someone will smile back.

Show your pearly whites today and feel the warmth of those who smile back.

Day 55

The Scapegoat

At some point during your grief journey, someone will push you over the edge emotionally concerning something that is entirely incomprehensible. This person's action inevitably causes you to lash out, releasing all your pent-up negative energy. I call this person (or group) the scapegoat, who unfortunately ends up in the wrong place at the wrong time.

For me, my bank was my scapegoat. The staff decided, without contacting me, to put a hold on my bank accounts when my husband passed, which caused me to miss monthly payments. When I inquired, the bank replied, "We read in the obituaries that your husband passed away, and it is our policy." I completely lost my composure and went on a tirade. Needless to say, the bank probably changed its policy that day.

My sister experienced her version of scapegoating when my mother passed away. Needing to cancel her doctor's appointment the next day, my sister contacted the doctor's office to explain her emergency. Rather than accommodating my sister's request, the receptionist insisted on charging a penalty fee for having canceled her appointment less than twenty-four hours in advance. Like I had, my sister gave the receptionist a piece of her mind without holding back.

Scapegoating is inevitable during your grief journey. Regardless of your inner strength and temperament, you will feel wrongly blamed or criticized for a given situation and react in a visceral fashion.

Day 56

Talk to Your Loved One

Visit with your loved one today.

- Share a cocktail.
- Tell a story.
- Bring flowers to the graveside.
- Look through a photo album.
- Reminisce about earlier years.
- Cuddle in a blanket.
- Watch a favorite movie.
- Write a journal entry.
- Set the table for two.
- Talk, talk, talk.

Day 57

Is There a Pattern for Grief?

Grief can often be defined in stages, giving the impression that your journey will be linear, finishing one stage and then moving on to the next, until you have accomplished all the stages. The stages of grief include:

- Shock
- Denial
- Anger
- Guilt
- Disorientation
- Depression
- Panic
- Acceptance

Unfortunately, grief does not work that way. There are no true patterns to grief. Not only is it not linear, it is also not circular. For some, their blueprint will be defined one day at a time. The early stages of grief may not be revisited, but most likely the middle to late stages will be reexamined multiple times. For example, immediately following a death you may feel guilty for not being at the hospital when your loved one passed. Later, you may feel guilty that you are the survivor who is fortunate enough to see your grandchild graduate from high school.

Day 58
Hope

As grievers, we continually look for hope—knowing that the emotional state we are experiencing will have a positive outcome.

We hope that someday we will be able to make sense of the loss and reengage in life in a happy and meaningful way. We hope that we will be able to transition the emptiness into being full again—sharing memories and creating new experiences. We hope that we can laugh and smile again as we once did. Mostly, we hope that our loved one's memory will forever be part of who we are and who we will become.

For many, finding the mentor who has walked a similar journey will be the key to finding hope. You can look at this person and say, "If she made it, so can I." You can, and you will find the much needed hope.

Day 59

Why Do People Run from Grievers?

I returned to work after a thirty-day bereavement leave and was stunned by how my coworkers dealt with my loss. At the time, I could not understand why they would run in a different direction when they saw me walking down the hallway, adding insult to my already injured soul. In addition, my peers didn't stop by my office to welcome me back to work and share their condolences.

Adding this burden of avoidance to the list of losses in my life since my husband had passed made me question the essence of my new existence. As I continued along my journey, I realized neither people in my neighborhood nor acquaintances at my daughter's day-care center made eye contact with me. I could not comprehend why people simply did not stop to talk.

The lightbulb went off in my brain many years later while working with a newly bereaved widow, listening to her share her discomfort with people around her. The distance from coworkers, neighbors, and acquaintances was not from a lack of caring; instead, the perceived coldness was the result of their not knowing what to do or say. Running from a griever is easier than saying the wrong thing.

As society continues to be educated in grief, we will all be equipped with tools that are helpful rather than hurtful.

Day 60
Cultural Differences

Dying, death, and grief differ among cultures. The beliefs, rituals, and customs have diverse meaning across different groups of people. Traditions surrounding death, funerals, and grieving among Latino, African American, Navajo, Hindu, Jewish, and Christian people vary based on culture.

Within these groups, observation of religious or cultural practices may vary based on an individual's belief. For example, the Jewish religion does not recognize cremation as a ritual, yet many individuals choose to cremate for a variety of reasons.

Discussion of cultural differences is important to help us be more tolerant of those around us who are grieving. Some cultures visit with the deceased's family before the funeral, while others wait until after the burial. Other cultures believe once the body has been buried it is time to "get over" the loss. Rituals are different among cultural groups, creating diverse ceremonies that include the burial, prayers, an open or closed casket, candle lighting, nourishments, celebration ceremonies, eulogies, and other observances.

Understanding how others grieve is helpful in your own grief. Open mindedness allows us to learn and accept different views.

Spend time researching customs and cultures of your religion and nationality. You will find it useful and comforting when looking for answers for what to expect during your journey.

Day 61

Creating Memorials

Creating a memorial honoring your loved one is a great way to keep this person's spirit alive with you, providing an opportunity to remain connected and reminisce. The memorial can represent a celebration of someone's life. The goal is to honor your loved one, while providing an outlet for you and family and friends to mark an important chapter in your life. A few ideas:

Things to Make

- Create a memory quilt using the clothes of your loved one. Make one for each family member. When it is finished, snuggle with it while watching television.
- Make a charm bracelet that includes hobbies or special dates (birthdays, weddings, anniversaries, vacations). Charms can be added in the future to blend life before and after the loss. Engrave the items with the dates or thoughts.
- Create a scrapbook. Use all the memorabilia you can find and write a story or caption by each picture or memory. Share it with family members and friends who may not have known your loved one. Keep it proudly in a prominent place.

Things to Do

- Design and plant a flower garden. You can even write your loved one's name using the flowers.
- Plant a vegetable garden. Grow your loved one's favorite foods.
- Create a blog to share with family, friends, and coworkers. Encourage them to add thoughts and stories. It's a great way to capture memories and share with others.
- Establish a scholarship fund in your loved one's name.

Places to Go

- Create a special memorial place in addition to or instead of a cemetery.
- Place a memorial plaque on a special rock, park bench, or brick. Be sure to visit it often and bring others to see it.
- Take a vacation where your loved one always wanted to go and never had the opportunity to visit. When you return, make a memory book to share with others.

Day 62
I Could Not Say, "He Died"

The words could not come out of my mouth. Saying he is dead meant it was over forever and he was never coming back. People died suddenly only in the movies and not in my real life. Dead meant he was gone forever.

I danced around using the words, probably to protect myself from something I have not determined yet. Using phrases such as "he passed," "he is no longer with us," or "he has gone to heaven" makes it sound like he may come back someday. The truth was, I was holding out hope.

Twenty years later, I can finally tell you he died.

Day 63
Today's Weather

Weather has such an impact on your emotional state on any given day. In grief as in the rest of life, how you embrace the weather has a direct impact on your day and your mood. It does not matter if it is raining or sunny, it only matters how you embrace what is given to you each day.

Sun—Feel the warmth of the early morning sunrise. Embrace the beauty of the rays as they shed light on the trees and dew on the grass. Grasp the warmth and place it in your heart.

Rain—Listen to the music of the drops as they hit your house, car, or umbrella. Create music from the sounds and sing a special song.

Snow—Watch the flakes as they hit the earth. Enjoy the cleanliness of the white flurries landing softly in your yard. Bundle up and play!

Wind—Feel the strength of the air as it hits your body. Capture the force and power, giving you the endurance to make it through each day.

Day 64

You Are Stronger Than You Think

Just as we say kids are resilient, so are adults. There will be days when simply getting out of bed might take all the strength you can muster. But somehow you rally. And you continue to rally day after day, working your way through the pain and making sense of the loss. Then one day you reach a point when you look in the mirror and say, "I am so much stronger than I ever thought I was."

Day 65
Reflection

Today is a day of reflection, a day to think about life—where you have been, where you are today, and what your future looks like. Today is a day to introspect and be thankful for all that you do have. Today is a day to look at the ones you lost with a feeling of happiness that you had time with them and not of sadness that they are gone.

Today is the day that the mirror image of your life is a reflection of what was and what is to come.

Day 66
Loss of What Was

What I miss most about losing my mom is the loss of what was. The loss of the Thanksgiving gatherings; the loss of calling her regardless of my emotional state, knowing she would calm me down; the loss of receiving an update of all our relatives in one phone call; the loss of the repeated stories; the loss of crafty gifts; and the loss of her.

While I truly miss my mother, I mourn the loss of what used to be, the familiarity and warmth of my life that was just humming along with the security of love, care, and understanding. Yes, we can rebuild by finding a new path, but what we really want is to have everything just as it was.

Day 67

Use the "Grieving Card"

Have you been in a situation lately in which you have had it up to your ears, and one more thing will push you over the edge? It's time to use the "grieving card."

A friend who lost her husband was at the airport in her car, waiting for her son who was at baggage claim. An airport security officer approached her, indicating that he would give her a ticket if she did not move the car. She used the "grieving card" by telling the officer she was recently widowed and that her son was flying home. Needless to say, he was a bit more lenient.

A mom who was consumed by settling her deceased mother's estate had missed the deadline for submitting her child's camp forms to the doctor. Not unexpectedly, the doctor's office informed her they would not be able to help her before the camp deadline. The mom used the "grieving card" and explained her situation, which resulted in getting the forms completed on time.

While it may not be the most comfortable situation for both parties, sometimes you have to share your emotional state, indicating that you are doing the best you can under the circumstances. Mentioning your recent loss may help ease an otherwise tense situation. And remember, use your cards wisely.

Day 68

Plan the Perfect Day

What is your perfect day?

My perfect day is a little "me" time: going for a run or hike, catching up on a bit of paperwork that is on my desk, visiting with a friend, catching up with my daughter, enjoying a great meal, and not overthinking anything.

While it does sound wonderful, to make it even better you have to shut off that part of your brain that is yearning to make sense of your loss and your new life. Often we go through the motions of having a perfect day, but the pain in our heart causes us to think too much, never allowing us to really relax.

Plan your perfect day today—calm your emotions so you can truly enjoy the day you have planned for yourself.

Day 69

Dreaming Your Loved One Is Still Alive

Have you been experiencing the recurring dream that your loved one is still alive? You wake in a cold sweat from a dream that seems so vivid and in the moment. You look around while trying to keep your wits about you, wanting to believe for a split second that the dream is true. However, as you regain your composure you realize that in fact it was only a dream, reigniting your mourning. When we dream of our lost loved ones, our brains are trying to find a way to deal with and come to terms with this most unthinkable situation. Sadly, these dreams are as much a part of the grieving process as tears are.

Embrace these encounters with your loved ones, but keep them in perspective.

Day 70
When Do I Get a Break?

Today!

Why does it feel like you never get a break from grieving? When grief takes on a life of its own and shadows your every waking moment, how do you get out of the grieving "pool" and come up for a breath of fresh air?

The key to this dilemma is to understand whether you need a break from grieving or a break from the tasks associated with grieving. Sometimes, the difference can be subtle and difficult to separate. So today, take a break from both:

- No writing thank-you notes today.
- No cleaning out the closet.
- No taking care of paperwork.
- No making lists of things to do.
- No talking about the hardship.

Instead, go to a movie, sit in the sun, read a trashy book or magazine, eat comfort foods, go for a walk, or just hang out in your favorite chair.

Day 71

What Is Your Glue?

Your glue holds you together each day when you
think you can't go another day dealing with the loss.
My glue includes:

- Family
- Friends
- Others who are grieving a similar loss
- Running buddy
- Book club
- Carpooling
- A great meal
- The sun
- Coworkers
- And don't forget the occasional glass of wine . . .

Find your glue.

Day 72
Grief Outbursts

What is a grief outburst?

An uncontrolled display of intense feelings usually caused by the griever's emotional state related to mourning the loss of a loved on. For some, the outbursts occur because of a trigger such as a movie, a comment made by a friend or family member, a family milestone, or just a bad day. These flare-ups are predictable and can be managed before they cause damage. The outbursts that take you by surprise are those associated with being easily agitated by something or someone that you were once able to emotionally control. These occurrences are less predictable and perhaps more complicated.

How to handle the outbursts?

When an outburst occurs, try not to respond immediately, walk away from the circumstance causing the distress, catch your breath, and try to calm down before responding.

Day 73

Never-Ending Self-Discovery

I often referred to my grief journey as an exercise of self-discovery. While I was mourning the loss of my husband, I was in fact learning about myself—often surprised by my strengths and overwhelmed by my weaknesses.

What I learned most was that I could survive the loss, carry on, and enjoy life again without my loved one. The self-discovery aspect of my journey was learning how to integrate my thoughts, emotions, and priorities into my new life. I discovered that I now had different goals with respect to my career and my relationships with friends and family. In other words, my priorities shifted based on my newly discovered personal findings.

Twenty years later, I feel as if my self-discoveries have shaped me into a person that otherwise I may never have become.

Day 74
What If?

If only we could go backward in time, before the diagnosis of the illness or the death, and rewrite the outcome—possibly saving the life of our loved one or possibly changing our behavior surrounding the situation.

We can spend the rest of our lives wondering "what if?" What if we ate better—would he not have gotten sick? What if I was driving instead of him? What if we never got on that boat? What if I had kids when I was younger? What if I took better care of my aging parents? What if I was more tuned in to seeing his emotional needs?

Obviously, speculating on the "what ifs" will not change the current outcome. While it is a natural behavior associated with a loss, repeatedly questioning or hoping for a different ending can be detrimental to your grief journey, as it is impossible to change the outcome.

Instead of spending time on the "what ifs," why not spend time on what you do have control over—working on changing behaviors for the future to ensure a different outcome.

Day 75
Connecting to Others

Find those people in your community that you can connect with personally. They may be people in your immediate circle who are grieving the same loss, or they could be people you have met through your grief journey who are walking a similar path. A few tips:

- Be open, friendly, and forthcoming with your loss. Be genuine and real. Others will share when you share.
- Trust the people you encounter with your story, your grief, and your new friendship.
- Respect their story, their circumstances, and their pain.
- Be honest without embellishing your story.
- Add value to the relationship—make it a two-way street.

Your new connections can be made at a support group, a religious gathering, or through an introduction by a friend. Embrace the connection!

Day 76

Can I Still Talk about My Loved One Who Passed?

Yes. Yes. Yes.

And everyone around you will or should listen. Many of us talk about our grandparents who passed away years ago, reminiscing about their cooking or sharing stories with great-grandchildren, so they have a chance to learn about their great-grandparents. If a father passes away when his child is young, the mother should share his characteristics and qualities with the child. If a child loses a brother, why not go through life knowing what he was like prior to his passing—did he like the same things? Was he a good baby?

For some, the notion of talking about your loved one could mean the griever is "not over" the loss or is in a "bad way." Actually, talking about a loved one is soothing, comforting, and a peaceful way of sharing the loss with others. For those who are concerned about hearing the deceased's name too much, start by determining if you are being too sensitive or if the griever is regularly talking about the person. If it is the latter, consider asking the griever carefully how she is and help her explore her emotions.

Day 77

Care for Yourself

The best advice I received during my grief journey was to be sure to care for myself in mind, body, and spirit. At the time, I could not appreciate this advice—let alone know how I would incorporate what I needed mentally, physically, or spiritually—as I could barely function.

In reality, the advice was great and very timely, as it provided the opportunity for reflecting on what I needed rather than concentrating on what I lost. I learned to make sure I was including activities that were helpful to my well-being, nourishment, and comfort.

Mentally, I was careful to surround myself with upbeat people and spent time reading to find a balance between what was and what is. I spent quiet time relaxing while listening to soothing music, providing me with comfort and relief.

Physically, I began a consistent exercise program and paid attention to what food I consumed, as it had a direct impact on how I felt. I also did my best to sleep regularly.

Spiritually, I spent time defining my outlook on loss and how it affected me on a daily basis. I contemplated my religious beliefs, what happens to loved ones after they have passed, and where I now fit into my new world. I found taking a walk, a bubble bath, or just sitting on a bench outside gave me the setting to reflect on what my needs were.

There are many ways to take care of yourself—determine what will help you succeed in your journey, and set aside time to nurture yourself.

Day 78

The Incomprehensible Truth

Incomprehensible truth is a phrase shared with me when I asked a griever several years after she lost her mother what was most challenging for her during the first year. She repeated that the loss was incomprehensible to her; she was not able to understand the realization that her mom had passed. She described the truth as the reality that the loss had really occurred.

Words to describe *incomprehensible*: *Unfathomable, beyond your understanding, deep, profound, vast, immeasurable*, or *perplexing*.

Words to describe *truth*: *reality, certainty, actuality, sureness, frankness*, or *candor*.

Day 79
Do People Really Think I'm Okay?

What do people really think when you walk into your office day after day following the loss of someone special? They ask you how you are, and you respond with, "I'm fine." Really?

Think of the same scenario for returning to school, attending neighborhood functions, or visiting your religious setting. People who have never experienced a loss have no idea what you are experiencing physically or emotionally. They can very well believe that you look good, so therefore you are feeling good. In reality, this is not true.

Here is the challenge: if you are honest by saying you are awful and having a terrible day, you have made it awkward for both parties. You may not want to share what you are thinking, but then they of course do not know how to respond. If you say, "I'm fine," and leave it at that, you are not being honest with yourself and those around you, creating the illusion that you are okay.

Choosing the path of least resistance is my recommendation—and choose that path based on the person and circumstances.

Day 80

How Should I Recognize Future Life Milestones?

Celebrate them.

For each grief milestone (monthly or yearly anniversaries, first birthday, first wedding anniversary)—find your inner strength to celebrate the event. The anticipation of the day will be more stressful than the milestone itself.

For each birthday—bake a cake, have a celebratory cocktail, attend a movie in a genre your loved one enjoyed, buy a gift for someone else, light a candle, cook your loved one's favorite food, or have dinner at their favorite restaurant.

For each anniversary—play "your song," reminiscence by looking at pictures and videos, reach out to your wedding party to reconnect, buy yourself a gift, or just be with your loved one by walking on a beach or sitting in your backyard.

Future family events—bring the memory of your loved one into the affair by telling stories, add a stick figure or picture to the family photograph representing your loved one, make a toast in his or her honor, or decorate with his or her favorite flowers or colors.

For life milestones ("lost" graduations, milestone birthdays, and children's weddings)—use the events as a way to continue to connect with your loved one in a happy and emotional fashion. Be thankful for what you had, not what you are missing.

Day 81

Favorite Memories

Our memories are our connection to our special person. Recall those exceptional times together and share them with others.

List five favorite memories you experienced with your loved one. Call five people and share those wonderful memories.

Day 82

How Long Does Grief Take?

Every book has a different answer to this question. Some say you must experience all the phases of grief before your journey ends, others say once you get through the "firsts" of everything you will be on your way to recovery, while others say the second year is worse than the first.

The true answer to the question is that your personal journey will define the timeline based on circumstances of the loss. Variables can include your relationship with the deceased, family dynamics, circumstances of the loss, current life situation, dependency on friends and family, and your own personality.

Take as long as you need, try not to compare your journey with others, and do your best to work on your grief rather than ignoring it.

Day 83

Remembering Grandma

A family of five adult sisters suddenly lost their mother when she was seventy. At the time, their own children ranged in age from six months to seventeen years. The sisters who had younger children were distraught that their children would not remember their grandma. One of the older sisters wrote a letter to the younger kids to capture the essence of Grandma:

Dear Matthew, Lauren, Nicholas, and Moira,

Your time with Grandma was cut short by her illness, and I am truly sorry for both you and Grandma, as I am sure your relationship together would have been filled with love, laughter, and wonderful memories. At the time of Grandma's death, you were too young to know her, so I want to share with you what a wonderful, warm person she was to everyone.

Her talents were many, and she had a fabulous reputation as a school teacher, was a loving wife and a caring mother, and she always bragged about her grandchildren—in other words, they could do no wrong. Family was the main focus of Grandma's life. The smile on her face when talking about family beamed to the moon. She and Grandpa were a great pair—always together and always smiling.

Grandma had many hobbies that included sewing, crocheting, doing crafts, cooking, and gabbing with everyone. She made the best seven-layer cookies, and the freezer was always full of cookies. As she would say, "You never know who could stop by."

With all tragedies come life lessons, and our family learned during Grandma's illness that she was amazingly brave and had more strength than we ever knew. She had a will to fight until the end, as she wanted to see her grandchildren grow up. The fact that your mom is now reading this letter to you means you are old enough to understand the loss of Grandma. While it is sad, stop for a minute, look at your mother, and smile, because the apple does not fall far from the tree, and you will see Grandma.

Love,
Auntie

Share with others your insights about the one you lost.

Day 84

True Pain

As a kid, falling off of a bicycle meant a scraped knee, a few tears, and a bruised ego. At the time, we said we were in pain. When we experienced a breakup from our first love, our broken heart hurt so much we thought we would die. At the time, we thought nothing could be more painful. For those who have given birth to a baby, the pain was so intense, but it was tolerable because you received a precious gift.

With grief, the emotional pain far outweighs anything we could think of physically. As a runner, I was fortunate to be able to turn my pain to physical exhaustion with the ability to run fast and long. People around me asked how I was able to push myself almost to the breaking point physically, and the answer was easy: physical pain goes away, but emotional pain follows you throughout all aspects of your daily life.

The key to pain is finding a sense of balance between the hurt and redefining your relationship with your loved one.

Day 85
Holiday Cards

Sending holiday cards triggers many emotional complications—if you have lost an immediate family member, addressing the missing person in the picture and/or the salutation poses an uncomfortable and often sad start to the already stressful holidays.

A different approach: send Thanksgiving Day cards instead of traditional holiday cards. This approach will provide you an opportunity to both thank those on your card list for helping you through the difficult days and to share how much you appreciate them in your life. Another idea is sending Valentine's Day cards instead of a holiday card. This method of holiday greetings allows you to share the love of your special person. Both approaches will allow you to connect with friends and family while not feeling the emptiness of the holiday season and the pressure to communicate during a taxing time of the year.

Day 86

They Become Saints

It seems as if most grieving people I have met share similar reactions toward their special person several months into their grief journey—they can't remember their loved one doing anything amiss. The deceased becomes a *saint*, but not in the religious sense. Grievers cannot remember any conflict, annoying behaviors, or bothersome issues between themselves and their loved one. Those things did exist, and everyone will admit it, but grievers lose sight of any of the less-than-tolerable behaviors.

I refer to this as a gift of grief—one of many that arises during the days, months, and years following the loss. Why should we remember the less-than-perfect aspects of our loved ones? Since they are gone, let's remember the wonderful aspects of life and love.

Day 87

Favorite Sayings

Gather your friends and family to help you capture the favorite sayings of your loved one. Recall those expressions that will fade as time goes by: the special way he or she described seasons, movies, family gatherings, and other people in your life. These unique sayings will always remind you of your loved one while bringing a smile to your face.

Day 88

Grief Is a Refuge or a Battlefield

I found grief to be a refuge, a safe haven where I could be with my deceased husband. I was protected from the outside world as I hid in my personal shelter with him— our sanctuary to be alone together where only we could understand the pain.

The world outside my sanctuary was like a battle-field. A combat zone of my own thoughts and emotions where I hung at the front line, being attacked by the people closest to me, hovering over me, wanting me to get out of the war zone.

We all need a refuge from our grief, but we need the battlefield to win the clash.

Day 89

Find Your Song

My funeral song was "Tears in Heaven," by Eric Clapton. I chose this song for my husband's funeral because I felt he did not belong in heaven, as opposed to here on earth with us, which the song highlights, but I also felt that he was crying from heaven and wanted to be with us. My "lost in grief" song was "Wish You Were Here," by Pink Floyd. My daughter and I constantly wished my husband was here with us, and we walked around many days as two lost souls.

My inspirational song that helped me be who I am today was "Colour of Your Dreams," by Carole King. The message of the song is that strength comes from within. Finding your will to carry on will help you get through the hard days and in the end it is all up to you. I played this song for energy before every race I ran, providing a connection to my husband.

What are your songs?

Day 90

A Broken Heart

Many country music songwriters find the perfect words to describe the feeling when a heart is broken. Most songs refer to a broken heart resulting from the breakup of a relationship between two people.

As a griever, a broken heart carries similar meaning when describing the pain. The survivor is left shattered, feeling defeated, traumatized by the loss, horrified by the experience, troubled about the future, and distressed by the situation.

The main difference is that you have not broken up with your loved one—you have the rest of your life to feel the essence of the person you lost, continue to be soul mates, and find compassion in knowing your loved one and the feeling of a continued bond. Embrace the spirit and mend your broken heart.

Day 91

Celebrate Your Loved One's Birthday By:

- Throwing a party
- Making a cake
- Eating a cupcake
- Going to an amusement park
- Taking a day off from work
- Having a cocktail
- Drinking a milkshake
- Blowing out candles, making a wish for each year you are celebrating
- Buying a present for yourself in their honor
- Volunteering at an event or organization in their honor
- Making a donation to a less fortunate person
- Singing a song
- Dancing on a table
- Making phone calls to those who are connected to your loved one
- Creating a memory to last until next year

Day 92
Write a Letter

Letter writing is an expressive way to release anxiety from your heart by placing your emotions on paper. Writing a letter is probably the best tool to articulate how you feel about your loved one or a person around you.

Letter writing encourages grievers to share emotional thoughts while expressing themselves in writing, including the good, the bad, and the ugly thoughts. Others use letter writing as a way of saying good-bye to their loved ones or sharing memories for future generations. Letters can be written to a:

- Family member
- Friend
- Your deceased loved one
- God
- Religious figure
- Doctor or hospital who cared for your loved one
- Hospice worker
- Neighbor
- Future grandchild

Once you know to whom you want to write a letter, it is time to get started. Many of us stare at a blank piece of paper or computer screen before we can begin, so the following are a few thought triggers to help you get started:

- I feel . . .
- I need to tell you . . .
- Please listen to what I am saying, I need . . .
- Since your grandmother's life ended too soon, I want to be sure you know all about . . .
- I am not sure how I will go on, but I do know . . .
- I think that you are . . .
- I have found support from . . .
- I have found peace knowing . . .
- I am angry because . . .
- I wish you could have . . .
- You could never understand . . .

Share your letters with others if you feel comfortable. Feel the weight lift off your shoulders as you express yourself in writing.

Day 93

"Share the Care"

There is no reason for you to carry all the burden when people want to help. Let others be there emotionally and physically to support you along your journey. Just as in the case of someone who is terminally ill, there is a lot of care that is needed when you are mourning the loss of someone special.

I would like to recommend a concept—developed in a book titled *Share the Care* by Cappy Caposella and Sheila Warnock (Touchstone, 2004)—to help organize a group to care for someone who is seriously ill. The concept is to put a practical system in place that includes friends, families, teachers, and coworkers to provide systematic support when you are experiencing a loss. By sharing responsibilities among a group of people, the griever will avoid overasking for favors, while allowing people to gain something personally by helping. Whether the tasks are to help clean out your parent's home, to carpool the kids to school, or merely to get a meal on the table, having an efficient and organized plan to tackle all the tasks will reduce the griever's stress level and help get all tasks completed.

Build your tight-knit circle to provide support for both you and your family.

Day 94

Morning Sunshine

Welcome each day with a new attitude, a new thought, or a new outlook on life. Consider it a day to recover and rebuild. Every morning creates a chance for starting something fresh with cheerfulness and happiness.

There is something about the radiating morning sunshine that offers a vibrant and crisp start to a new day. The freshness of the air and the rays shining through the trees makes for a tranquil and peaceful way to endure what is in front of you.

Find peace and calmness through the serene and beautiful sunrise each day.

Day 95

No Place Is Untouched by Grief

Do you wish you were a bug that could hide under a rock, so no one could find you? Or a prairie dog that could climb into a hole for safety?

Unfortunately, no place in your life is untouched by your grief. The constant reminders show his or her face at every turn. And around every corner is the realization that you experienced a wonderful loving relationship with the special person you lost.

Be sure to hide when you need to escape your surroundings in order to protect yourself, but continue to search for the places that provide strength.

Day 96
Inner Strength

Inner strength is an essential component of you—it is the fire within that allows you to accomplish all that you want to achieve in life, the willpower to believe that you can succeed in all you attempt to conquer, a power that helps you thrive even in the most difficult situations.

Following the loss of a loved one your inner strength is challenged, leading to self-doubt about your survival. Your emotional toughness will provide the source of support needed to get back on track.

A young mother once shared with me that, after the first anniversary following the loss of her mother, she did not think she would be able to sustain the pain of losing her mom. At the time, her youngest child was seven months old, and, before her mom's passing, the two had spoken every day. When asked what helped her get through the darkest days, she said her inner strength—which she was unaware she had.

Light your fire!

Day 97

Reevaluate Your Needs

In earlier readings, we talked about the need to take care of yourself through eating well, sleeping regularly, and exercising. At the beginning of your grief journey, the basics are what sustain you through any given day. As your journey matures, your needs will change based on returning to work, attending school, maintaining the daily needs of your family, and, most important, taking care of yourself.

Now might be the time to add some entertainment to your life by getting out of the house more, visiting with others, or attending an event. Maybe you need to formulate a goal with milestones to get you excited about a future endeavor, or maybe it is time to just sit in the shade outside or by a fire reading a book. Whatever you believe your needs to be, that is where you should invest your time.

Day 98
Accept Silence

Silence is golden: a proverbial saying, often used in circumstances where it is thought that saying nothing is favorable to speaking.

Spending time in sheer quiet and stillness allows you to retreat into your own space. Often the audible sounds around you are from people telling you what you should be doing and how you should be doing it. What you really want is stillness, allowing yourself to engage at your speed and apply your agenda.

Accept the peace of silence while staying calm and at ease.

Day 99
Find a Buddy

The special pal who will be there no matter what type of mood you are in—the person you can trust with your innermost thoughts, emotions, and your sorrow from grief.

These are the buddies who will stand by your side as you walk your journey through grief. There is plenty of room in life for multiple buddies, as a one-size-fits-all comrade will not fulfill all your needs. You might have a buddy who you can talk to who really listens, you might have a buddy who will exercise with you, or you might have a buddy who shares an interest in food. You might even have a buddy who will attend a support group with you or help you clean out the closets.

Search for your special friends who will be there for you through the tough days.

Day 100
Allow Yourself to Laugh

It might be time to allow yourself to laugh at yourself, a television show, or a story that your friend or family member has shared with you. Set aside your grief for a moment and engage in something that is amusing.

If it has been a while since you really laughed—engage in a cackle, snicker, or flat-out giggle. The people around you will be thrilled to hear you laughing. After all, laughter is contagious.

Day 101
Nature and Grief

Today, experience the beauty of nature, the tranquility of the natural forces of the earth and its inhabitants. Feel the circle of life and how all aspects fit into an ecosystem far greater than humans could have created.

Experience the day from start to finish based on your natural surrounding.

Watch the sunrise, hear the birds chirp, examine the flowers as they open from the cool night, listen as the wind blows through the trees, and watch the sky cloud up as the rain approaches.

The natural gifts of life will help you heal from your loss.

Day 102
Finding Religious Support

For many grievers, religion will play an important role in their recovery, while others will lose faith in their religion as a result of their loss. Your religious journey through grief may include one or the other—or possibly a combination. For those who did not practice faith in any religion prior to the loss, religion may now provide much-needed support.

During the early days of grief, grievers often look for answers to help reduce the pain and suffering. Based on religious beliefs, many find comfort in believing God will provide support in an afterlife. Having a strong faith with commitment to your religious affiliation will provide strength and encouragement throughout your journey. Embrace your congregation and those around you who are lending a helping hand spiritually.

For those who have a lesser connection to religion, try not to overanalyze why you feel the way you do. Instead, find an association or organization with less religious emphasis. Embrace family traditions and cultural beliefs, or simply connect to a group of people who can help you.

Religion is interpreted as a collection of beliefs, cultural systems, and worldwide views of humanity in relation to moral values and spirituality. Define your own religion that can help you through your special journey, and find the appropriate support.

Day 103
Tears

Tears are a natural and physical reaction to strong emotional stress, anger, suffering, mourning, or physical pain. Some tears are controllable, while others catch you by surprise, based on your emotional reaction to the circumstance.

Just as a smile shows a positive emotion, it also expresses a reaction to something that makes you feel good. A tear can also be a reaction but is often interpreted as worrisome. Crying and the shedding of tears can actually make you feel better, as they are releasing emotional energy that can otherwise become distracting.

In my presentations and support groups, I encourage the attendees not to fight their tears but rather to use them as a way of releasing their anxieties, connecting with their loved ones, and expressing their current emotional states.

Day 104

Concept of Griever's Toolbox

All projects need tools to get the work done.

If you are creating a photo album, you need a book, pictures, cutting device, decorations, pens, and glue. These are the tools necessary to tell a story. If you are training for a 10K running race, you need running shoes, appropriate clothing, race registration, a running plan, a running watch, and nourishments. Again, these are the essential tools to successfully run a 10K.

To effectively work through your grief, creating a toolbox will provide you with the resources and supplies you need to make it through each day. A few examples of what could be found in a griever's toolbox include:

- Tissues
- Grief books and articles
- Journal to write your daily thoughts
- Calendar of important dates
- Pictures and stories of your loved one
- Family and friends
- Support group
- Personal counselor
- Workplace
- Religious beliefs
- Pet(s)
- Exercise plan

Most toolboxes contain customary resources that are essential to completing the project; however, with grief the tools will change over time. Therefore, create your own toolbox and add new tools as you discover them.

Day 105
Meditation and Yoga

Some days, the idea of escaping from your grief is just what the doctor ordered. The notion of escaping does not imply you are avoiding or ignoring emotions associated with your loss, it simply means you are taking a much-needed break. Why not take a break by meditating or taking a yoga class?

Meditation is an inward-oriented practice, in which you induce yourself into an internal state of reflection or compassion, centering on a specific focal point. Meditating provides an opportunity to be with yourself in a positive and emotional place where personal thoughts are pondered, considered, and mulled over. The practice is a form of relaxation, where you can escape from your harsh emotions while providing an opportunity to clear your mind.

Originating in ancient India, yoga is a physical, mental, and spiritual practice for the purpose of relaxing your body to improve health. The system of exercise associated with yoga provides a platform to stretch your muscles, using breathing techniques that result in calming yet physical exertion. The best place to practice yoga is in a peaceful and tranquil environment, offering your body a chance to rest and relax and resulting in a more positive mental outlook.

After meditating or attending a yoga class, you will be that much more relaxed and stronger to take on your grief again. Make it a weekly break!

Day 106

Ways to Support Grieving Children

As adults, we ponder the best approach to help grieving children. We have a tendency to hover and overanalyze their behaviors, not knowing if they are acting out because of grief or simply because they are children. We want to give them space, but we want them to talk to us as well. We consider their distance as a form of grief, but they are digesting what has happened and, just like us, are unable to articulate what they are thinking or what they need (no different from adults). Here are some tips to help children who are grieving:

- Answer their questions truthfully. Being honest in the end will help all parties involved.
- Be available to answer their questions when they are ready to ask them. Answer them directly, using words the child can understand.
- Use the deceased person's name when referring to their loved one.
- Talk with them about the person who has passed. Share memories and stories.
- Be accepting of sadness, tears, and anger. Let the child share all their emotions.
- Show them your emotions—let them know you are hurting as well.
- Acknowledge and share special days together. Let them decide how the day will unfold.

Day 107
Find an Angel

In an earlier entry, I asked who your angel was, and if you didn't have an angel, I asked that you try to find one.

An angel is that special person in your life who has held your hand and guided you through the toughest days of grief. The person whom you trusted with your emotions and who helped provide the courage you needed to get through to the next day. The person who was honest with you and did not beat around the bush when sharing his or her opinion of how you were doing.

As you continue your journey, continue to search for those special angels who protect you while guiding you through the next chapter of your grief. These new angels can provide not only wisdom from experience but can also provide the motivation to take the next leap in your journey. Find the angel who has walked a similar walk, who will provide hope that you will make it—that you will survive and that you will live again.

Day 108

Seasons of Grief

With each season of the year, your grief will find a new significance. Seasons are similar to being a subdivision of the year marked by changes in daylight, weather, and environment. Grief has its own journey similar to animals and plants—grief will hibernate, migrate, and become dormant as the earth rotates and the sunlight changes. Each season provides an understanding of anticipation, change, and desire.

Spring is the time of year dedicated to rebirth, renewal, and regrowth. Trees bud with new leaves, the wildflowers bloom in the meadows, and the grass turns green. The smell of the blossoms and the freshly cut lawns trigger memories of our childhood and the final days of school before summer break. The afternoon rainstorms are our tears of loss making way for a rainbow to watch over us.

Summer is the time for longer days filled with sun, heat, and humidity. Fruits and vegetables are juicy and sweet, and you can feel the sand between your toes as you walk at the beach. Summer provides the opportunity to barbecue with friends and family while reflecting on the wonderful aspects of the life you shared with your loved one. Share fireside stories, cook delicious meals, and be reminded with each mosquito bite that your loved one is right there with you.

Fall brings crisp air, the turning colors of the foliage, and harvesting of fruits and vegetables. It's a great time of year to be outside, set goals for the new school year, or bake your favorite pie with newly picked apples. The rustling of the leaves under your feet is a reminder that life has cycles, as does grief. Put on a sweater, find a rake, and scoop up the leaves, enjoying the sound of them crunching under your feet. Reflect on your journey, your loved one, and the constant changes of the seasons and your grief.

Winter is time to snuggle with a blanket, book, and hot cup of tea. It's the time of year to hibernate, when the days are shorter and the temperatures drop. There is nothing better than the pure whiteness of a snowflake falling from the sky or the puff of your breath from the cool temperatures. Although both winter and grief are often perceived as sullen, take this special season to spend more time with your loved one: create a memorial, organize belongings, and reflect on a wonderful life together.

Day 109

Managing Your Stress Level

It's easier said than done. Not really.

- Cut out the things that don't matter.
- Avoid the people that are irritating you.
- Find a stress reducer: exercise, bath, glass of wine.
- Leave your work at work.
- Take a break from routine.
- Order dinner in.
- Return the phone call tomorrow.
- Let the dishes wait until you are ready.
- Smell the roses.

Day 110

Embrace a Family Project

Make it a project for all your family members, regardless of age, ability, and availability. Come together and decide as a group what the project will be, pick a team captain, and work out specific roles, so everyone has a responsibility. Project ideas could include:

A house project—Pick a room that as a family you spend time in. Freshen it with a new rug or new paint colors, clean off the bookshelves, organize the cabinets, or rearrange the furniture. Make it a group decision, and enjoy the new space as a family.

Clean out a closet—As a family, decide what you want to do with your loved one's personal items. Do you want to leave them alone, pack them to reminisce later, or divide the items you want to save and determine who should get what? Be sure to share stories you remember regarding a special piece of jewelry, tie, or toy.

Create a memorial—Make this a memorial that all family members can participate in creating. Plant a garden, make a DVD of photos, find a special place to visit and adorn with a plaque, capture your loved one's life of stories in a journal, or build a shrine.

Embrace a hobby of your loved one—
Choose a hobby that your loved one enjoyed participating in and embrace it as a family. No piece is too
small or too big—dabble in it and pass it down to
the next generation.

Day 111

Don't Sweat the Small Stuff

Don't spend energy solving the challenges you don't have control over. The silly things that can set you off are often out of your control.

- Instead of worrying about the weather— embrace it!
- Instead of complaining about traffic— sing a song!
- Instead of stressing over what to cook for dinner—purchase it!
- Instead of concerning yourself with what people think—do your own thing!
- Instead of worrying about getting the laundry done—wear something else!
- Instead of returning a phone call—take a walk!

At some point, everything will get done that has to be done—don't sweat over the smaller challenges. Save your energy for the bigger items that need your attention.

Day 112

Be Honest

Often when we are grieving the loss of someone we love, we waffle in our thoughts and beliefs. While we are truly distraught over the loss of someone we care about, we are willing to do anything to feel better, including embellishing how we feel and how we are progressing in our grief.

Remaining honest with yourself and those around you will allow you to work through your grief, while defining your future. For example, if you feel it is time for you to move the picture of your husband from next to the bed, the gesture is one of sincerity and a genuine step to help you through your grief. If you want to clean out your little girl's bedroom because the visual of the empty bed is too distracting, be honest with your feelings, as you will feel more comfortable with your decision. If family members sit down to talk to you about how you are getting through the days, answer with truthfulness—including the good, the bad, and the ugly. They will appreciate your candidness, and you will feel better for sharing.

There is nothing to regret if you are honest. If your fear is that others will judge you, then they are being dishonest to themselves, as they have no idea what it is like to walk in your shoes.

Day 113

Why Don't We Get Along after We Lose Someone We Love?

Being a survivor after the death of someone who has been a part of our lives will change us forever. We formulate our own personal opinions of what the person meant to us, how we want to proceed in life, and how others will fit into our master plan. The challenge is addressing all the other survivors who are creating their master plans.

Truly, it is not that we don't get along anymore with others. Instead, as individuals we have come up with different survival paths, leading us to judge each other's actions. We expect people to think and behave the same way we do, even if they are not capable. We embrace the theory that actions speak louder than words, and when we don't understand our friends' and family's actions, we think they don't care or they are not grieving—when actually they are just behaving differently.

To get along with each other, we need to embrace that we grieve differently, we express our thoughts differently, and we love differently.

Day 114
Teddy Bear

Teddy bears are the most useful grieving tool ever. They come in all sizes, colors, and shapes. They are cuddly, cute, and love you unconditionally. They can represent your loved one in name and personality. They don't care if you cry or shed tears on them. They are always smiling, even when you aren't.

Get yourself one, and dress it in an outfit symbolizing a hobby of your loved one. Sleep with it or place it on a shelf. Take it in the car with you or leave it on the couch to greet you when you come home. Buy it a playmate—someone to hug while you are away.

Call it your "bear-eavement bear."

Day 115
Rediscovery

Your loss becomes a time for rediscovery, emotional awareness, and redefinition of your life. Where to begin, what to discover, and what needs to be redefined will all be an outcome of your grief journey. You will rediscover along the way what the wants and needs in your new life are, what is important, and what needs to be resolved.

Embrace the emotional ride, be aware that a rediscovery is occurring, and be patient to discover the most suitable outcome.

Day 116
Returning to Work, School, and Church

Reengaging in a routine will have a variety of reentry points as you work through the first couple of years of your loss. At first, your emphasis is getting back into a routine with your community. Reentering physically—getting your feet wet but not really diving into the water.

As time goes by, your emphasis will shift to emotionally pursing reentry—putting additional effort into your job, your education, or your congregation. Striving to feel a part of the team rather than standing on the sidelines. The reconnection will help you find your place once again—feeling good about yourself and reconnected to life.

We all need something to return to—it is essential to feel wanted and needed.

Day 117
Finding Comfort

For most, finding comfort comes from places that are easy to access. Gentle words from a friend, an open ear, or a compassionate touch can help you get through the day. Find that special person in your life who can help provide comfort, reducing the discomfort associated with grief.

Day 118

Giving Thanks Every Day for What You Do Have

For many, grief is an all-consuming emotion. The survivors are consumed by the death of a loved one, resulting in overwhelming sadness of losing what they once had—and often losing sight of what they still do have.

I watched a young mom on Mother's Day who was so distraught over the death of her mom that she was not able to celebrate, yet she had two young children who wanted to make it special for her. The conflict within us creates inconsistencies in behaviors and our subsequent reaction to life.

Logically we know that we have so much to be grateful for in life—including our health, family, friends, careers, children, homes, and community—yet emotionally we only feel what has been taken away from us.

What if every morning we woke up by enjoying the sounds of the birds chirping, felt the morning's cool air, and watched the new sun rising. Write down three things to be thankful for today, and remind yourself of what you do have rather than what you have lost.

Day 119
Treasure Your Memories

After the loss of a loved one, what remains are the years of memories created together in love, friendship, and understanding. The culmination of the special outings, experiences, and bonding moments are stamped in your brain and heart forever.

Now is the time to embrace those memories while cherishing the time you were able to spend with your loved one. Relish in the intimacy of the relationship while appreciating the value of your experiences. Be sure to share the pictures and stories with future generations, making new memories that will last for a lifetime.

Day 120
Making a Quilt

Making a memorial quilt using your loved one's clothing is a perfect way to remain connected physically. Having the quilt to wrap around you provides you with the ability to stay connected while reminiscing with the visual of each of the quilt's squares.

Start by sorting through the closet and searching for those special items from your loved one's hobbies and memorable occasions. Create a pile of the clothing that you would like to include in your quilt, and choose your loved one's favorite color for the border. If you are creative enough to make your own, start cutting the squares needed to make the quilt. If you prefer someone to make it for you, search the Internet for a seamstress or company that will make it for you.

The final product will be something you can cherish forever, whether you hang it on the wall for decoration or wrap yourself to feel the physical touch. Multiple quilts can be made for family and friends. A great family project!

Day 121

Empathy versus Sympathy

Empathy is the ability to understand another person's feelings or to be compassionate toward someone who is hurting.

Sympathy is a feeling of sorrow for another person's pain and suffering.

Often, friends and family members who are experiencing a loss with you share empathy, mourning the loss of a special person together. People who are slightly removed will have sympathy for you and your loss, as they are not experiencing the same emotions firsthand. With empathy, two people can be walking in similar shoes and can relate to the difficulties and hardships of a loss. Two widows who collaborate on parenting or discuss challenges with in-laws have great empathy for each other. With sympathy, a nonwidow will have sympathy for a widow but cannot relate directly to the experience, providing a different type of emotional support.

To help with your grief journey, surround yourself with both empathy and sympathy, which will allow you to relate to some and receive love and support from others.

Day 122
The Deceased

Today is a day to reflect on the deceased: Those special people in your life who are physically gone. The ones you are unable to touch or create new experiences with but are able to connect with in memory forever.

Reflect on where you believe they are spiritually, what you would say to them if they were alive today, and how life would be different if they were sitting next to you reading this entry. As the days go by, it is often challenging to remember what life was like having them sitting next to you or being just a phone call away if you had a question. While we miss them tremendously, they unfortunately miss out on future experiences. It is therefore our responsibility to include them with a song, their favorite food, a gesture, a story, or a special thought, so we know they are sitting right next to us.

Day 123

Ruts

Denver is a town that relies on solar removal of snow following a snowstorm. Since the chamber of commerce claims there are three-hundred-plus days of sunshine a year, this seems a reasonable solution. One winter several years ago, Denver received thirty-six inches of snow. And because the side streets were not plowed, huge ruts formed, causing travel down those streets to be challenging, as cars would slide in the ruts.

Since a rut is a depression or groove worn into a road or path, isn't that the same as our grief path? If we allow ourselves to be in a rut or get stuck, we agree to that awful feeling that we're waking up in the same spot day after day, emotionally and physically not being able to climb out of the rut or carry on.

How do you get out of the ruts? By not allowing yourself to navigate down the road that provides obstacles you can't steer away from. Avoid them!

Day 124

Band-Aids

In my early months of grief, I relied on finding Band-Aids to fix everything around me. I would try to counteract the pain by finding a simple solution that an adhesive bandage could solve. My wounds would be dressed by placing the Band-Aid over my pain, and it would go away.

Unfortunately, the Band-Aids were not the answer to my pain but rather a way to hide the wounds, preventing them from healing. Finding joy again allowed me to remove the Band-Aids I was using as a crutch to get through the days.

Day 125

Communicate Your Wants and Needs

A *want* is something you would like to have but can live without; a *need* is something you must have to survive. While dramatic in nature, the concept conveys a system to determine what it is we want and what it is we really need.

You have your "village" circling around you, wanting to offer support and guidance as you walk your grief journey. While you search for your wants, be sure to let them be supportive of your true needs. Communicating your needs will allow you to create and define the wants.

Life is meant to be lived, not just survived. Treat yourself to some extra wants, both emotionally and materialistically. Let the feeling that comes from indulging give you a boost of strength to get you through to the next phase of your grief.

Day 126

Learn to Delegate Responsibilities

It is time to create the list of responsibilities that have been pushed aside since you experienced your loss.

For example, if your loss is a parent, it might be time to get the legal affairs in order, empty the home, and sell it. This may require coordination between siblings, specific timing of tasks, and extensive planning. Don't feel you have to take it all on yourself. Collaborate on a list of what needs to be done, in what order, and the appropriate timeline—then delegate each task. Be patient, so your family members can be successful in accomplishing their responsibilities.

If you recently lost your spouse and have dependent children at home, you probably have been operating from a list of what *has* to get done while everything else has been neglected. It may be time to engage your children. For example, if you cannot drive the car into the garage due to clutter creep that has taken over that space (toys and boxes with your loved one's items), you can engage the family in getting organized. The kids will love to help by deciding what to keep and to find the best places to organize the belongings. Delegate who does what, and reap the rewards as a family.

Often we avoid getting back on track because the tasks are so overwhelming that the thought of where to begin derails the process. Learn to make a list and delegate the responsibilities to others who will help.

Day 127
The Warmth of a Hug

The special embrace of two people offering love, affection, friendship, or sympathy shows support and comfort; the warmth of being held by someone who cares often changes your perspective on the day, offering much-needed strength.

A hug of more than two people is referred to as a group hug.

Find someone who will reach his or her arms around you, squeeze you tight, making you feel loved and that everything will be okay.

Day 128

Would You Rather Have the Years Cut Short or None at All?

A college friend lost her son while he was in high school, a loss I could not wrap my arms around no matter how hard I tried to imagine what it would be like—even after spending fifteen-plus years supporting grieving individuals.

The father stood at the podium and delivered an amazing message to friends and family attending the funeral:

> So God asked Sue and Mark, "Do you want to get married? It will be hard." We said, "Yes," and he said, "I am going to give you a beautiful son and beautiful daughter, but the catch is that your son will only live for sixteen years, seven months, and twenty-four days. Do you still want him?"
>
> Sue and I looked at each other and said . . .
>
> "You gimme that boy!
> You gimme that boy!
> You gimme that boy!"

As you work through your own grief, isn't it true that you would rather have had your loved one in your life, regardless of how long or short, rather than never have had that person at all?

Day 129

Bad Days. Good Days. What Is Today? Let's Make It a Good Day!

After reading today's reflection, turn around all the "bad" thoughts you have for the day and really work hard on making it a good day. Reach into your griever's toolbox for the strength to look at everything surrounding you as half-full rather than half-empty. Interpret comments from friends as thoughtful and your task list as doable. Be thankful for what you do have in your life.

Day 130

Climbing a Mountain

Think of your grief as climbing a mountain. Visualize yourself standing at the base with your backpack on your back filled with all the necessary gear to make it to the top. You have the strength to accomplish this hike, so you start climbing. Along the way, the steepness slows you down, making you want to turn around, but you know in your heart you can do it. You reflect on why you want to accomplish the feat and what it will actually take to achieve your goal. You stop along the way for nourishment and rest before tackling the next milestone. When you see the summit, you know your desire to accomplish the challenge will carry you the rest of the way. As you crest the top with a feeling of triumph, embrace the emotions and the knowledge that you can conquer anything.

Continue to push through the pain and reach the top!

Day 131
Timeline for Healing

Healing is an ongoing process that takes time, energy, and the desire to feel well. How long this takes will truly depend on the circumstances of the loss, your personal makeup, and the people in your life.

Daily reflections provide insight regarding the importance of not rushing grief by accepting support from others around you and the inevitable ebbs and flows of what each day will bring. As you progress through your journey, you will be able to accomplish milestones, knowing that you are moving emotionally through a nondescript timeline.

As a griever, your timeline for healing should take its own unique course—one that you experience both emotionally and physically without a set schedule.

Day 132
Light a Candle

There is something magical about the flame that is associated with a candle. The way it sways with the movement around it; the way it changes when it touches the wax; or the colors that come from within the blaze. A candle allows us to safely stare at a fire and lose ourselves in thought. We often light candles to share a special occasion, in memory of a loved one, or for spiritual connections.

There are many uses associated with a candle: celebrating a birthday, decorating a dinner table, relaxing in the bathtub, or providing scent in a room. Light a candle tonight and enjoy the enchanting feeling of serenity.

Day 133

Memories Are Comforting

Our experiences with our loved ones are forever engraved in our hearts. The special times we had together are memories we can find comfort in forever.

While I lost my husband at a very young age, I will forever have the memories of our baby being born and find comfort that we experienced the early days of parenting together.

As a daughter, I will always have the memories of my mom, who paved the road, teaching me how to be a parent. I find comfort in raising my children from the memories of my childhood with her.

As a granddaughter, I find comfort in baking rugelach yearly in memory of my grandmother, who took pride in rolling each piece. I cherish the memories and the smells of my kitchen, reminding me of her teaching me how to bake.

Find comfort in the memories!

Day 134

The Treadmill of Life Continues, but I Fell Off

Treadmills are an amazing piece of equipment that you can run or walk on. Regardless of your speed, you maintain a forward momentum. The belt provides a soft landing for each foot, and the electronic controls allow you to set the speed and elevation that is appropriate for your fitness level.

Now imagine the same treadmill is your life, filled with drive, thrust, and energy. When one day you lose someone close, and the treadmill of life continues, but you don't have the strength, willpower, or determination to hang on—you fall! The belt continues to rotate and the treadmill continues to move, but you are no longer on it. The fall causes a few scrapes and bruises that will eventually heal, and someday you will find the strength of mind to get back on the treadmill and rejoin life!

Day 135

Find Your Temporary Cave

A father shared this story after the death of his son. He created a room over the garage as a sanctuary where he spent time with his son. He moved all of his son's belongings into the room and displayed them. The father found solace in this newly constructed cave he built where he could be with his son.

A young widow shared the story that she joined a summer pool club in the next town over from where she lived to avoid running into people she knew. Every evening after work she picked up her daughter from day care and went to the pool. The mom spent hours in the baby pool with her daughter, listening to people around her sharing what a great mom she was for sitting in the pool every evening. What they didn't know was that the pool was her cave, her way of getting away from others who would not understand.

Caves are places where you can crawl into and hide—not forever, just temporarily when you need to be alone.

Day 136

Do at Least One Thing You Enjoy Every Day

Make it a priority today to do at least one thing you enjoy. Put aside your grief, the ongoing list of emotional concerns, and the feeling of loneliness.

Find pleasure for you, enjoy how it feels, and find something new for tomorrow.

Day 137

Don't Ignore Your Grief

Ignoring your grief is often a common thread among people who have lost someone they love—hoping that someday they will wake up and it will go away. The truth is, grieving is a longer journey than we expect. As the days turn into months, some grievers find it easier to push away their grief rather than to face it head-on.

Ignoring your grief lends itself to relying on a crutch to help you through your day. It is not uncommon for grievers to depend on alcohol as a means to release anxiety and relax, while others become totally absorbed in work or exercise. Anything in moderation is great; however, any sign of excessive behavior is an indication to regroup and reconsider a different path. The wounds need to heal— and they will—but ignoring that you are grieving is not the best approach.

Day 138
Sorrow

Sorrow is the feeling of deep mourning caused by a loss suffered following a death—a sadness that cannot be described in words but only felt in the heart. Sorrow is a word that clarifies exactly to friends and family the true hardship of the loss. You are sad!

Being sad, filled with sorrow, is a natural reaction to loss. We will always carry sadness when we mourn the loss of someone close, but how we interpret and embrace the sorrow will guide the journey.

Day 139
Waves

While sitting on the beach watching the waves from the ocean, I thought about grief and how it comes and goes just as the waves do.

And like grief, waves are a natural flow with no specific pattern. There is energy associated with the breaking of each wave as the water hits the beach, forming a vacuum as it retracts back to the ocean. As a storm surges, the wind will change the force of the waves, making them more turbulent and powerful.

Doesn't that describe the ins and outs of grief? Just like waves, grief is so powerful that it can knock you off your feet, but when the water recedes you can stand back up.

Day 140
Look Good, Feel Good

Whoever coined the phrase "look good, feel good" was spot on. When you get up in the morning, take a shower and make sure you choose an exceptional outfit, putting extra effort into getting ready—you will have a much better day. Once you are dressed, look in the mirror and take joy in what you see.

If you look good, you will project the feeling that you are feeling good.

Day 141

Capture the Stories

Each of us has so many life stories to share. Some of the stories are good, while others are bad. Some are funny, while others are sad. Some are interesting, while others are boring. And some are long and involved, while others are short and sweet. It doesn't matter what the topic of the story is as long as you capture it in your mind and heart.

Now is the time to ask everyone around you to share a story about the person you recently lost. You will be amazed at how much you learn about your loved ones through the eyes and hearts of those they touched. Reach out to neighbors, friends, schoolmates, coworkers, distant family members, a coach, a religious leader, and your immediate family. Hearing the stories will warm your soul and at the same time allow you to reminisce about a life cut short.

These stories can also be captured in writing and published as a book or recorded as a video. Regardless of the media, the purpose is to capture the stories and share them with those connected to your loved ones.

Day 142

Be Tolerant of Your Physical and Emotional Limits

Today is different from yesterday, and tomorrow will be different from today. The key is to be tolerant of where you are on any given day. Being aware of your physical and emotional limitations will help you avoid discouragement.

A key consequence of grief is not being capable of performing at your best. To avoid dampening your spirits, learn your limits and be tolerant of your current threshold. If you're tired, sit down and put your feet up until you feel rejuvenated. If you are having trouble concentrating, take a break and do something comforting to help with your emotions.

You will bounce back—and next week will be different from this week. Hang in there!

Day 143

Life Isn't Always Fair, but It Does Provide

Great memories, compassion, and a lot of love. No one ever told us that life would be fair but rather that it would be fulfilling.

During your difficult days, try to concentrate on what you do have. Fairness is in the eye of the beholder, and to be fair one would have to be free from bias or prejudice. We often look over our shoulder to see what others have that we don't have—instead, look inside to see what you have, and you will see more fairness than not.

Day 144

Go to a Movie

Lose yourself in a movie theater chair. Buy popcorn and indulge in 120 minutes of entertainment and a break from life. If you want a good cry, see a movie that will allow you to shed a few tears. If you want to be emotionally lost, go to a movie that is action packed. Whatever the genre, sit in the dark, immerse yourself in the experience, and take the much-needed break from life.

Day 145
Whom Should You Trust?

Trust everyone who has been standing by your side and providing support since the loss of your loved one. If they did not care, they would not hang around during the more difficult days of grief. Whether they are family, day-care providers, your banker, or a neighbor, they are with you because they care about your well-being. While they may not understand exactly what you are going through, trust that they will be as honest as possible when helping you with a personal challenge, financial issue, or when they are just being a sounding board.

Day 146

Personal Belongings—Next Step!

Move forward only if you are emotionally ready. Enough time may have gone by to start considering what to do with your loved one's personal belongings. You may not be ready to clean out the closets yet, but maybe you can think about what you want to do with the groupings of personal items.

For example, are there certain people who would appreciate the tools or sporting equipment? Is there a nonprofit that would benefit from the clothing? No need to sort through anything yet—the goal is to start thinking about where the items would be useful when you are ready to divide up the personal belongings.

Day 147

Where Have My Friends Gone?

They have gone back to their daily activities and responsibilities. While you may feel as if they have deserted you physically, they have not in their hearts. Your friends have returned to carpooling, vacationing, parenting, and their normal routines. The difference is that your normal routine has changed, and you feel the void.

Remember, your friends don't know how you are feeling on a daily basis, so be cautious about taking it personally if you don't hear from them as often. To help with the void, ask them for help. As a friend of a griever, there is nothing more fulfilling than being asked for support. They are just a phone call, text, or email away.

Day 148
Worrying Is a Waste of Time

Worrying is those emotions and thoughts that are perceived to be negative in nature, usually caused by agonizing over or dwelling on something. As a griever, worrying is not uncommon, as it is a way to engage in the "new normal" in your life. You may worry about dealing with finances, taking care of your elder parent, meeting all your responsibilities, or taking care of your home. It is rare that a grieving person does not worry about something.

There are physical expressions of worrying—biting your lip, pacing back and forth, or bouncing your leg up and down while sitting. These are a physical reaction to your emotional thoughts. If you can determine what is making you anxious and find a remedy, you will have less distress, which will allow you to use your energy for more productive activities.

Try not to waste your time worrying.

Day 149
Gift of Life

Life is not a gift tied with a pretty bow. While it is a gift, it is up to us to find the box, wrapping paper, and bow to create a happy and productive package. Your relationships with friends and family are to be shared with love— sometimes there are obstacles in the way and the box gets dented, but in the end, the gift of knowing the one you lost is all that matters.

Day 150
Grief and Anger

Often grief and anger go hand in hand. Most grievers will experience some type of anger when they lose a loved one, even if they have not been wronged. I vividly remember throwing my husband's belongings in the bedroom because I was so angry that he had passed away. Of course, he had nothing to do with his passing, as he died of natural causes.

The challenge with anger is that it often causes resentment, fury, and rage, which does not bring your loved one back and only adds to the stressful situation. At the beginning of your grief journey, anger can be helpful in getting you through each day, providing a vehicle to challenge your emotions. As you proceed through your journey, however, anger has the tendency to hurt your progression, as it is can cause negative thoughts and energies.

Day 151

What Would Your Loved One Want You to Do?

As much as we feel guilty for laughing or carrying on after we have lost a loved one, we know in our hearts that our loved one would not want us to suffer. Yet we still shy away from reengaging and enjoying life. There is something about being the survivor that shapes our journey—maybe because we have the opportunity to enjoy life while our loved one is now missing out on the opportunity.

Your loved one would want you to be happy, be in love, and enjoy new experiences. Until we as grievers can turn the switch off in our brain and realize it is okay, we often find it difficult to reengage. Try to imagine if the roles were reversed—we would never want our loved one to stop living.

Day 152

Same Dream,
Finally a Different Outcome

Why is it that we experience the same dreams night after night? When I lost my husband, my recurring dream was seeing him standing in the driveway when I returned from work. He was standing there waiting for me to get out of the car, and it seemed like nothing ever changed in the dream. Each time, I woke up sad, confused, and lonely.

After months of experiencing this dream, one morning I woke up realizing I had dreamed about memories that we shared together and had a feeling of fulfillment and love. I can't tell you when this happened—it just did, and I treasured my nights of sleep rather than panicking that I would wake up with that recurring emptiness.

Day 153

One Meal a Day Should Be with Others

Eating three meals a day alone can be lonesome. For some, a magazine or book might satisfy the feeling of being abandoned or deserted, allowing you to enjoy your meal at your leisure. That is all good for a short period of time.

As time rolls on after your loss, however, it might be time to share a meal with others, which will provide companionship and camaraderie. There is something to be said about having a conversation with others while eating, providing an opportunity to share your day, discuss a current event, or just feeling loved, which adds continued hope following the loss.

Reach out to friends, family members, or colleagues for one meal. Enjoy your newspaper with breakfast, but allow lunch or dinner to be more social.

Day 154

Remembering Health, Not the Illness

For those of us who have been caregivers or have watched loved ones suffer with a disease for a long period of time, it is often difficult to remember spending time with them when they were healthy, vivacious, and enjoying life as they so deserved.

A common observation from those who have watched friends or family members suffer is that you only remember the illness. You have a visual of them losing weight, not eating, or spending the majority of their day in bed. The complicated emotion is that we really want to remember them healthy, but it has become problematic, as our visual memory is of the illness.

This is the time to share stories, to look at old photographs and movies that express the strong and fit person you knew before the illness. Try to change the image of the sickness and remember the healthy days. By sharing with others, you can remember the happy and healthy times and allow that to become your new visual footprint.

Day 155
Fear and Avoidance

Why is fear such an active emotion when dealing with grief? We fear what others think, we fear that responsibilities are falling through the cracks, we fear for what our future looks like, and we fear that our behaviors are not normal. Fear is a natural reaction to grieving the loss of someone you love. We agonize over making decisions and are apprehensive to interact with others when we are fearful.

So how do you manage fear? Avoidance. Most grievers will dodge anything that conveys a feeling of anxiety. What if for today and this week, you challenged yourself to conquer one fear by not avoiding it. It can be cleaning out a closet, writing a note, returning a phone call, committing to a vacation, spending time with a friend, tackling death-related paperwork, or going after the next complicated item on your list. Break it down into smaller pieces, so you can feel your accomplishments along the way.

Day 156

The Changing Colors of the Leaves

Each year as summer turns to fall, the leaves on trees and bushes become majestic shades of red, yellow, and orange, leaving the green of summer behind. While the days get shorter and nights get cooler, we are reminded that life has cycles. Leaves begin as buds and grow to green leaves before changing colors and falling off the tree to start a new cycle next spring.

Just like leaves, life has cycles—buds represent birth, green leaves represent life, vibrant colors represent changes, and leaves falling off trees represent loss. As we grieve the loss, we must remember that there will always be new buds.

Day 157

Time: Does It Really Heal?

A griever once asked me if time really heals the empty feeling of the loss of someone you love. This is a difficult question to answer, as I believe time does not fully heal the loss, but time *does*:

- Soften the pain
- Connect you with your loved one
- Help you to appreciate what you do have
- Let you bond with others associated with your loved one
- Provide you the opportunity to reflect
- Allow you to evaluate your life since the loss
- Let you remember all the special moments together

Day 158

Individual versus Group Counseling

Try them both.

Individual counseling provides you with a one-on-one encounter in which you can privately share your thoughts with a counselor. You can create your own agenda and remain on task regarding what items you would like to discuss and receive support on.

Group counseling provides you with a group setting guided by a facilitator with a preplanned agenda or topics provided by the attendees. In a group setting, members can offer insight into their personal journey, providing an opportunity to connect with others who have walked a similar walk.

If you find an individual counselor you do not connect with, try another one. If you find a group that does not gel for you, find another one. Once you find the right fit, make the connection and visit often.

Day 159

Finding a Support Group— Dos and Don'ts

If a group setting is right for you, be sure to follow a few guidelines.

Dos

- Find a group that is specific to your type of loss. If you are widowed, being with other widows will be helpful.
- Find a group close to home—your attendance will be more frequent.
- Find a group that meets in a location you feel comfortable with: lighted parking lot, easy parking, comfortable setting.
- Attend knowing that you will be open and honest with your thoughts.
- Listen to others; their experiences (good and bad) will be helpful.
- Be patient with others in the group.

Don'ts

- Keep from judging others—we all experience loss differently.
- Make sure not to arrive late or leave early.
- Avoid talking on top of others.
- Don't take up all the time with your story—let others share.

Day 160
Believe in Miracles

Whether you believe in Santa Claus, the Easter Bunny, or that the Red Sea parted—your special divine intervention is what you need to help you experience your special "want." Create the energy and believe in miracles.

Day 161

Start a Home Project

For grievers, weighing how much time to spend at home versus time away from the house is often a fine balance. When you are home, start "nesting" by starting a home project. The endeavor will make you feel good about your space and feel a sense of accomplishment. A few ideas:

- Redecorate a room.
- Paint your house a different color.
- Rearrange the furniture.
- Buy new furniture.
- Learn how to fix your leaky faucet.
- Update your landscaping.
- Organize a closet.

Day 162

Stepping Up to the Plate

There are some days when you have to step up to the plate even when you feel as though you don't have the energy. A few thoughts:

- If kids don't go to practice, they can't play in the game!
- If you don't buy groceries, you won't eat well.
- If you don't go to work, you won't get paid.
- If you don't take your medication, you won't get better.
- If you don't study for the test, you won't pass the class.
- If you don't pay the bills, you won't have electricity.
- If you don't hug a friend, you will feel alone.

Step up to the plate today and erase your "don't."

Day 163

Filling the Hole

The absence of a loved one feels as if a hole has been drilled in your heart that will be impossible to repair.

Start by finding a patch—a small token or break allowing you to have good days along with your bad days, as well as finding the much-needed strength to make it through each day. With each patch you will find power and passion to slowly fill the hole in your heart and learn to live with the loss while having the strength to go on.

Day 164

Religious Beliefs

Religious beliefs play a significant role in an individual's grief journey. For some, answers are found in the griever's connection with their religion, congregation, and God. For others, simply being connected to rituals, traditions, and customs while grieving provides comfort and understanding.

Frequently, grievers experience emotional conflict between religious beliefs and mourning the loss of a loved one, especially if it was a sudden or tragic death. Often they are looking for answers to questions that really don't have answers.

In my continued journey of helping those who are grieving, I have come across many grievers who struggle with an inner conflict relating to their religion. As time goes by, these conflicts will resolve themselves with either a new path or a restoration of their faith.

Day 165
Zipper

There are many metaphors for grief—some more common than others, some more realistic than others. Recently, while working with a griever, we had a conversation about how a zipper could be a good representation of grieving a loved one.

- The closing of a zipper connects two people as the teeth interlock.
- The opening of a zipper represents being pulled away from your loved one.
- Increasing or decreasing the size of the opening enhances or restricts the passage of emotions.
- Adorning the zipper represents your colorful life with your loved one.
- A broken zipper is hard to mend, just as a broken heart is.

The mechanical wonder keeps our loved ones with us, so pull up your zipper and connect with your loved one.

Day 166
Finding a New Hobby

The time has come in your grief journey to take on a new hobby or activity. The new pursuit can act as a diversion that will take time and energy, allowing you to redirect a portion of your emotions of grief to something of interest and growth.

Start slowly to ensure interest and avoid overcommitment, choose wisely to fulfill an interest, and involve others for support and encouragement. A few ideas:

- Take a cooking class and then invite friends or family for dinner.
- Plant a garden, starting with research to see what grows in your area.
- Participate in an athletic activity with a goal to take part in an event.
- Volunteer at a school or nonprofit organization.
- Join a book club.
- Redecorate a room in your home.

Day 167

The Funny Moments

With each tear comes a great deal of laughter. List five
of the funniest times you spent with your loved one. As
you reminisce the shared moments and wonderful laughs
together, cherish the funny moment. Share the story with
others and laugh out loud, resulting in happy tears.

Day 168
Trust Your Instincts

Your instincts will guide you; they always have and they always will. Your heart might be hurting, and your brain may not be operating at 100 percent, but your instincts will be there to help guide you through your grief journey. A few suggestions for how to trust your instincts:

Constructively question your surroundings and decision making while grieving, but in the end trust your gut to make the best decision. Once you make the decision, go with the flow and don't second-guess your decision. You can revisit it down the road.

Listen to your inner voice, something only you can truly understand. The voice will guide you—ask questions, but use the answers received as input. In the end, you know yourself the best.

Reflect on how you reached this place in life. Capture the good to take forward with you and the bad for learning purposes. Channel the reflections as you move forward to guide your instincts.

Trusting your instincts will empower you to walk the necessary journey in front of you. Most often you will make the right choice, but when you don't, you will continue to learn what is right, and your internal compass will continue to lead the way.

Day 169

An Estranged Family Member

Being estranged from a family member is often the result of a perceived hostile, unsympathetic, or indifferent circumstance, resulting in alienation and removal from an accustomed association.

For some, this may occur many years before a loss of a loved one. In fact, the loss can bring the family back together, triggering to forgive and forget the alienation that caused the separation. In this case, it is important to remember each individual is different, and the success of rebuilding the relationship will depend on not labeling and passing judgment on others. Most important, know that people communicate differently, express grief in different ways, and make different lifestyle choices. Often, estrangement is caused by not understanding one another, which can result in judgment.

For others, the estrangement comes following the loss of a family member, often caused by the reaction to the loss, the care provided in the last few months, or information that is discovered after the loss. The estrangement is a way of separating oneself from the pain associated with others' opinions and gestures. It is not uncommon for a family to disagree on care, the funeral, or the estate, causing further estrangement of a family member. However, taking care of yourself is most important, and as time goes by, you can attempt to repair what has been broken by the loss.

Sometimes it is inevitable that the relationship cannot be repaired, but for the most part, time may provide the ability to forgive and forget. Carrying resentment, anger, and missing out on lost opportunities often are more tiresome than actually repairing what has been broken.

Day 170
The Perfect Griever

Is there such thing as a perfect griever? If so, find me the perfect griever, so we can all learn how to grieve efficiently and effectively. We are not sure we will ever find such a person, as we will all grow from our grief and make mistakes along the way. Regardless of the path we take, we will become our own perfect griever. Have faith in yourself and your journey.

Day 171

Join a Support Group

It might be time to connect with others who are walking a similar path.

A preconceived notion that a support group is a place where you sit around in a circle discussing sad and dreadful topics while watching others cry, and then you walk away more depressed than when you walked in, is just not the case.

I facilitated a twice-monthly widow support group for seven-plus years, servicing hundreds of young widows suffering a loss. As I watched the attendees over the years, I was amazed by their growth and determination, learning from their experiences and watching them enjoy life again. I am not sure they could have accomplished reentry into life in such a positive and productive manner without each other. They shared survival tricks, how to engage with others, and how to survive an ordeal that only they can relate to.

The openness and honesty of discussions in a group setting empower grievers to take the steps needed to help with recovery. Here, they share with others who "get it," who will not judge them, and who will never tell them it is time to be "over it." Learning how they have overcome obstacles, how they have integrated the loss into their current lives, and how they have learned to smile again is priceless.

Join a group today—when you feel confident about your journey, hang around and help support the new attendees by providing hope through your experiences.

Day 172

Take Time Off from Life

Even before you experienced your loss, there were days when you wanted to take time off from life. Having the ability to turn off your brain and your emotions and just enjoy your morning coffee, watch the sunrise, and listen to the birds without planning or worrying about your day is a great start for taking time off from life.

If only we could take time off. If only we could spend the day reading, sitting by a pool, or going for a hike in the mountains without being concerned about anything. If only we didn't have to worry about finances or hurting someone's feelings. If only the kids could take care of themselves for one day. If only the house projects would get done.

Complicated by the loss, taking time off from life seems impossible. In reality, however, it is not impractical to close your eyes and let everything disappear for a moment or an hour. Actually, taking time off from life will help you tackle what is in front of you. Take the much-needed break and ask for help in getting your daily responsibilities done as you come up for air.

Day 173
The Ocean

On a recent trip to the beach, I sat back and pondered the notion of grief as it relates to the ocean. I found myself mesmerized by the natural surroundings of the experience and how the ocean has its own circle of life.

I watched how the ocean reacts to storms, creating waves and undertows, while the sand moves with the rising and lowering of the tide, and how the shells surface on the beach, reflecting the life of what once inhabited them. The seaweed reveals the plant life under the sea, and the salt smoothes the sea glass, creating soft lines.

The ocean is complex, dependent on all life matters to create the natural life cycle under the sea. Isn't that the same as our life? Complex, needing both life and death to create a true circle of life.

Day 174

When in Doubt,
Take One Step at a Time

Stop to reflect or analyze, but be sure to continue taking steps one at a time. Today is about placing one foot in front of the other while feeling confident about your decision, your direction, and your ability to walk without reservation.

Just one step at a time!

Day 175
Take a Class

When is the last time you studied something other than for a class in school or a project for work? Maybe it is time to sign up for a class that embraces an interest you have always wanted to pursue but for which you never took the time.

Possibly an art class to help express your creativity, a literature class to help immerse yourself in reading and interpretation, or a photography class to capture new life experiences. Maybe it is time to learn more about home maintenance and remodeling or creating a garden.

Whatever class you choose, be sure not to let the schedule create additional stress or hardship, but do accept the opportunity as a commitment to yourself, your well-being, and desire to embrace a new adventure.

Day 176

Balance of Old and New

Your emotions are probably similar to a seesaw; applying weight in one direction can tip you one way, but which direction would you prefer?

Working through your grief is a delicate balance between your old existence and the building of your new way of living. Finding the equilibrium where you feel comfortable. Knowing the old at this point might be more desirable but actually impossible to obtain, as your loved one has passed away.

Finding the balance between old and new will rely on your ability to reestablish your relationship with your loved one, so as you continue with your new life you merge the old and new. You are who you are because of the relationship with your loved one and your experiences associated with the loss.

Incorporate all you have learned and unite them together in your definition of new, creating a much-needed balance.

Day 177

Peer Support versus Professional Support

Peer support refers to support provided by people who are of equal standing with you—those who have experienced a similar loss but do not have formal training in grief care. The support provided by peers is based on knowledge gained from a loss and ways they have overcome the challenges by living with the loss on a daily basis.

Professional grief support is support received from people who have been trained in the field of grief. They have knowledge of the phases of grief, expected behaviors, and ideas to help you with forward momentum as you work through your grief. What they don't have is personal experience of what you are truly experiencing.

For you, finding someone you can relate to, someone who understands, and someone you can ask honest questions of is most important. Whether it is in the form of a peer or professional, you have to find the connection. What works best is a combination of both peer and professional support, as this will provide different perspectives—both so helpful during your journey.

Day 178
Employment

Employment can be a blessing or a curse to some grievers, depending on the emotional and physical needs fulfilled by a job. There are good reasons to work while you are grieving the loss of someone you love, but for some, the challenges associated with work are too stressful. The emotional and physical needs met by being employed include:

- Financial requirements
- A place to go every day
- The feeling of commitment
- A temporary mind eraser
- An opportunity for a success
- Passion for the work you are doing

The stresses of being employed include:

- No longer caring for the type of work you are doing
- Not having the motivation to perform at your normal proficiency level
- Too many people pulling you in different directions
- Not being able to juggle all your responsibilities at home/work, creating more stress

Creating too much change early in your grief is not recommended; however, finding the balance of providing income as necessary while determining what you want to do with your career is important. Meet halfway: take the time you need for grief while maintaining a sense of fulfillment in your work.

Day 179

Learn Your Boundaries— For Yourself and Others

Your personal limitations change with a significant loss. What you were once tolerant of may actually become the thorn in your side, the level you once performed at might decline slightly, and your ability to cope with certain situations may diminish.

With that said, your personal boundaries of caring and understanding toward others may have increased with the changes in your priorities and surroundings. The important aspect to remember is your boundaries will change as your travel through your grief journey. Some will be permanent while others will be temporary adjustments, allowing you to work through your needs.

Be aware that not only are your boundaries shifting through the loss, so are those of the people around you. Some want to help you recover faster, so they may step into your arena; others back away, not knowing how to react. Family members may try to move your boundaries, suggesting what you should or shouldn't do. Try not to close the door on them but rather communicate where you have established the border around your grief. Be sure to let them know when you shift the border to allow more room for them to enter back in. Like most aspects of grief, changes occur along the way.

Day 180
Bake a Cake Today

Dig out the cookbook, search through your cabinets for ingredients, and turn on the oven. Today is the day you will make your house smell wonderful, indulge in something delicious, and reminisce, having cake and tea with your loved one.

Freeze the leftovers and pull them out when you want to reconnect.

Day 181

Ten Ideas toward the Road to Recovery

1. *Find a new hobby.*
   - Grow a garden.
   - Work on a craft.
   - Join a book club.
   - Take a cooking class.

2. *Perform volunteer work.*
   - Honor your loved one by volunteering at a nonprofit.
   - Read to children at an elementary school.
   - Volunteer your time at a cultural event.

3. *Establish employment.*
   - Reenter the workplace.
   - Find a job that makes you feel good about yourself.

4. *Take a class.*
   - Sign up for an art class.
   - Dive into a literature class.
   - Study a new topic.

5. *Attend a cultural event.*
   - Buy season tickets to a community theater.
   - Attend a lecture at a local university.
   - Visit a museum.

6. *Establish a well-care program.*
   - Exercise.
   - Eat three well-balanced meals a day.
   - Spend more time outside.

7. *Support fellow grievers.*
   - Spend time with those who are grieving, which can also help your grief.
   - Help newly bereaved individuals.
   - Lead a support group.

8. *Create a home project.*
   - Redecorate a room.
   - Rearrange your furniture.
   - Organize your closets.

9. *Join an organization.*
   - Attend a religious group meeting.
   - Become a member of a town- or school-board group.
   - Participate in a book group.

10. *Spend positive time with friends and family.*
    - Plan family outings.
    - Meet friends for lunch.
    - Make new friends.

Day 182
Envious of What Others Have

Often what we see is not necessarily what it appears to be. Unfortunately, when we are grieving the loss of someone close, our first reaction is to be envious of others, as we can fabricate in our heart and soul what appears to be a perfect scenario.

If you are widowed and you see a married couple, you may become resentful. If you are a grieving parent and see a family, you may become spiteful and jealous. If you see adults with their aging parents and you have lost both your parents, you may dream of one more day together.

As you travel through your journey, try not to judge a book by its cover—you never know what is lurking in the pages. Be conscious of what you do know, and that is that you miss your loved one, and therefore you are envious of what you see.

Day 183

The Sun, the Moon, and the Stars

Look to the skies as you move through your grief journey.

The sun will warm your heart, as it rises and sets each day. Reflect on the brightness it has shed on you, and build strength from its heat.

Observe the phases of the moon as it orbits the earth. Start when the moon is only a sliver, and each night the reflection will grow until the moon is full and shining down on you to guide you through your journey.

The abundance of stars in the sky will shed light on an otherwise dark time in your life. The illumination will change just as each day will change as you make sense of your loss.

Walk outside each day and look up to the sky for strength.

Day 184

Find an Analogy for Your Grief

Using a physical analogy of your emotional grief can help provide a visual that may support you with your journey. Visualize your grief as:

- Chiseling away at rock
- Melting an iceberg
- Climbing a mountain
- Crossing an ocean
- Seeing the light at the end of the tunnel

Day 185

Create a Well-Care Program

Taking care of yourself both mentally and physically is extremely important when grieving the loss of a loved one. Creating a well-care program will allow you to engage in good choices for yourself, your health, and your grief. A few ideas:

- Spend more time outside.
- Eat at least three meals a day.
- Change your cooking habits.
- Get better and more sleep.
- Spend time with friends and family.
- Splurge on a massage.
- Develop an exercise program.
- Organize your daily activities.
- Obtain knowledge through reading.

Day 186

Cry with Someone

Finding someone to cry with tends to be more healing than crying alone. Being with anyone who understands your grief and can relate to the loss provides comfort.

Sharing a cup of coffee or a glass of wine with someone you connect with is important. Allowing yourself to be free with your thoughts by not holding back, asking questions, sharing concerns, and generally having the opportunity to be sad together is helpful. As you bond, you will share tears of sadness but also tears of joy.

A good cry is one of the gifts of grief: the great feeling after releasing your emotions.

Day 187

What Is Your "Aha" Moment?

The special moment of clarity when something clicks as if magic has occurred. Where you can gain wisdom changing your outlook on life. Your moment can be a sudden understanding, recognition, or resolution of something that has not been clear in the past.

How do you know when you are having an "aha" moment? Your heart might beat a bit faster, the lightbulb may turn on in your head, and you might feel your eyes have been opened to something new. Whether big or small, sad or funny, your "aha" moment can be surprising and inspiring.

Cherish your moment of clarity, whether it is of your loved one, a family situation, or life in general.

Day 188

Grieving Your Future

As a griever, not only do we grieve the loss of our loved one, we grieve the apparent loss of who we were and the future that has changed from the loss.

Day 189

Postpone Major Decisions

The majority of grief books you read will tell you to postpone any major life decisions in the first year of grief, and I would have to agree. (Of course, this applies only if you can put off having to decide now.) These decisions include:

- Changing your job
- Moving to a new home
- Moving to a new city
- Getting married/divorced
- Having another child

As you walk your journey, decisions you make today can impact the road ahead for you. While it might seem like the right decision at the time due to your emotional state, it might end up being a greater hardship later. For some, financial situations will drive making a change, but even then, try to hold off until you can logically address the change.

Day 190
Find Your Rhythm

Grief has a mind of its own. It takes control at times when you least expect it, often catching you off guard and leaving you in an emotional state. The best way to take control of your grief is finding your own rhythm.

Learning how to react to the sudden burst of grief comes with practice, just like playing a musical instrument. Over time you will find your special tempo, adjusting to your life changes and finding the beat that works for you.

Day 191
Paying It Forward

The expression "paying it forward" can be used in many contexts, and in the case of grief, it is used to describe the notion of repaying the support you have received by supporting others who are following behind you, experiencing their own loss of a loved one.

You may think you are not in the place to support the next round of grievers, but in fact it will be a win-win situation. By helping them you are providing wisdom and experience, and in return you receive reinforcement of how far you have come in your own grief journey.

As a fellow griever, I am thankful for those who held my hand through my early days of grief, and while I cannot offer them the same support in return, I can provide hope to the next generation of grievers.

Day 192

See the Milestones of Your Progress

When we are grieving the loss of a loved one, we become so enthralled with our emotions and current state that we often lose sight of how far we really have progressed since the initial loss. Along the way many milestones have been reached, confirming progress that is frequently overlooked.

Remember the days when you could not eat a meal, sleep through the night, or even drive a car? Or when you spent the day crying and never smiling? Yes, we still have those days, but they are not constant. And don't forget the days when you could not finish a thought, recall what you were looking for, or didn't have the strength to return a phone call.

Mark the milestones as growth and understanding of the process. Remain positive as you progress through your journey, and appreciate how far you have come by looking forward into the horizon.

Day 193

Grief Has No Face

We walk down the street every day and drive in our car taking notice of people around us. On a good day, we might wonder where they are going, where they have come from, and what their life is about. In our society, people watching has become a sport.

Human behavior is fascinating, and until you have experienced a loss you may never have considered the reason why people behave the way they do. In fact, you get agitated when someone cuts you off driving or bumps into you while walking—without ever thinking it might be because they were preoccupied with grief.

Grief has no face. In previous generations, grievers wore black clothes or special hats. Today, if you do not know the people, you would have no way of knowing that they are struggling through the day just as you are.

Day 194
Mutual Giving

To get through a day after I lost my husband, I felt like I was continually asking for favors. Whether it was asking my boss for a couple hours off from work to take care of an important meeting or asking my neighbor to help fix a problem at my house or asking day care to forgive me for being a minute late for pickup. For a griever, this is a setback, as you are reminded that you can no longer operate as you once did.

A friend helped me find a solution for some of my anxiety. She introduced the notion of mutual giving, which really eliminated the stress of asking for a favor. On Wednesday evenings we would take turns caring for each other's daughters, so two nights a month I got a break and two nights a month she got a break. This gave me the opportunity for a night off without cashing in a favor, as I would be giving to her the next week, so she could have a night off.

I used the concept with others, allowing me to give, so I could receive.

Day 195
Daily Changes

For some, when we lose a loved one we immediately think of how this will affect us logistically on a daily basis. How will the day look if I cannot have breakfast with my husband? Who will take care of Dad now that Mom is gone? Who will teach my kids family traditions now that Grandma has passed?

We cannot change the loss, but we can modify our desire to have similar outcomes by approaching the situation differently. Maybe you change the way you eat breakfast, possibly working out first or packing breakfast in a cooler and eating at work. You can care for your dad by putting a family schedule together to help, or you can hire a service to be with him during the day. As for teaching family traditions—you can teach them!

Deal with the changes by finding a solution that works, tackling one challenge at a time.

Day 196
Belly Laugh

When is the last time you belly laughed—you know, the type of laugh that made you believe you might wet your pants or made your eyes tear?

Scan YouTube for a funny video—laugh until you cry. It feels great!

Day 197

No One Is in Charge of Your Happiness but You

How many times have people told you that you are responsible for your own happiness?

We know it but still find it difficult to grasp—even more difficult is finding happiness after a loss. People can project happiness on you through compliments, affection, and caring, but ultimately it comes from within. Grievers search for happiness in many ways:

- A deeper connection to their faith
- Reconnecting with family members
- Engaging in self-care
- Finding a new hobby
- Volunteering for an important cause
- Engaging more with family members
- "Nesting" at home
- Finding comfort foods
- Indulging in retail therapy
- Believing in you!

Continue to search for happiness, and regain the confidence that you will work through the pain.

Day 198

Finding a Companion

There is something about having a puppy that can make anyone smile. Of course, training the puppy is a different topic.

If you are not ready to take on a pet, consider finding a companion through supporting a service dog or caring for a friend's pet while he or she is away.

Like anything else in life, a new pet can be a challenge, but I continue to receive wonderful feedback about how caring for a new pet offers companionship, changing the griever's life.

Day 199
Remaining Open to the Concept of Hope

Hope is an emotional state in which you believe a positive outcome can occur relating to an unfortunate circumstance caused by events in your life—in this case, despair caused by the death of a loved one.

Remaining open to the concept of hope means you are willing to and desire the achievement of a positive outcome. The timeline and circumstances surrounding achieving the desire may be flexible; however, knowing that the direction you want to move in, while having reasonable confidence that it will occur, is the first step.

Day 200

Regardless of How You Feel Today

Get up, get dressed, and show up.

Try it for today; push your emotions aside and conquer today with passion, meaning, and oomph. You can do it!

Day 201
Embrace Music

Whether it is listening to a song on your iPod, playing a musical instrument, or singing, let the melody move you—get lost in the sounds of the instruments and the lyrics of the music. Embrace the harmony, study the chords, and enjoy the pleasantness of the music.

Find a comfortable place to listen and sit back, relaxing and taking pleasure in the sounds.

Day 202

Being Thankful for What You Do Have

When I asked a friend, who was grieving the loss of her husband, what she had learned about herself through the loss, she responded, "I am constantly thankful for how much I *do* have. I don't think I'd be as appreciative of my kids, health, friends, family, and more if I hadn't lost my husband."

Why does it sometimes take a life setback to realize what we have? It is interesting to note that her kids, health, friends, and family had always been in her life. However, while revisiting the relationships after her loss, she realized there is a lot to be thankful for. While losing her husband was horrendous, appreciating what she has will assist her in moving forward.

Day 203

Realizing Who in Your Life Really Counts

Another great lesson learned regarding friends and family when you are suffering a loss is realizing who really counts. There was a time when the number of people who reached out to you on a daily basis or the invitations you received was an indication of your popularity or importance. How times change.

With a loss, you realize you don't need a lot of people in your life—just a few very supportive ones. Experiencing a substantial loss makes you realize who is really in your life and whom you can actually count on.

Day 204

Remembering Your Loved One

Remember your special person every day. There are so many ways to get positive energy from your loved one simply by engaging in normal life. Refrain from the sadness while embracing the wonderful memories. Here are a few suggestions:

- Flip through special photos.
- Stroll through their favorite park.
- Eat at their favorite restaurant.
- Call a relative and share a story.
- Shop at their favorite store.
- Partake in one of their hobbies.
- Mimic one of their gestures.
- Cook their favorite meal.
- Rummage through their personal belongings.
- Watch home movies.
- Visit their favorite museum.

Find your special way of remembering your loved one.

Day 205
Support Fellow Grievers

Although you would prefer to be an expert in something other than grief, your experience provides you with knowledge that can be shared. This wisdom allows you to be extremely helpful to newly bereaved individuals.

Even if you feel as though you can barely take care of yourself, by engaging with recent grievers you will have the opportunity to open your heart to help while proving to yourself that you have come a long way in your own grief journey.

Newly bereaved individuals will ask simple questions, wondering if what they are experiencing is normal. You will know the answer to that and so much more. You can be a guiding light, and grievers will flock to you for a special hug.

Day 206

Wearing Your Shoes— Not Someone Else's

Wouldn't it be easy to jump into someone else's shoes to avoid having to mourn the loss of someone you loved? If only you were able to avoid grieving by climbing into a different pair of shoes.

Actually, by putting on your own shoes you will be walking your own journey, experiencing the complexities of grief, tackling the difficult challenges, and embracing the fact that you have lost someone you love. If no two journeys are alike, the notion of wearing someone else's shoes really means you are avoiding dealing with the loss. Piggybacking on someone else's experience might sound like an easy way out, but in the end it only means you are not addressing the loss.

Find your comfortable shoes and embrace your own journey.

Day 207
Read, Read, Read

As the days go by after your loss, you might find yourself being more focused and able to start reading again. While your attention span may not be exactly where it was before the loss, you might be able to sit a bit longer to read and absorb the words.

Immediately following the loss, you probably were rereading the same sentence over and over again, not absorbing the words. Now might be the right time to embrace a book that you will be able to get lost in. Try to choose one that will keep your attention, with subject matter that provides a break from your grieving. Also, the book should not be too long, allowing you to finish it in a timely fashion.

In addition to losing yourself in a novel, read any-thing you can find on grief. You will be amazed at how far you really have come when you read experts' opinions and what others are experiencing. The exercise will provide you with an emotional boost, erasing the feeling that you are alone in your grief.

Day 208
Talk, Talk, Talk

Talking about your loss and your feelings is by far the best medicine for working through your anxiety. Talking provides an outlet to release your thoughts, and hearing yourself talk provides a channel for you to make sense of where you are and where you want to be.

Sharing your concerns will allow people around you to help and comfort you, since they will know what you are thinking and feeling. As you listen to yourself talk, you will realize all the wonderful memories you have captured with your loved one before his or her passing. You will be able to prioritize what is important and what can wait, allowing you to redefine your life.

Keep sharing the stories—people want to hear them just as much as you want to tell them.

Day 209

It's Okay for Your Children to See You Cry

How can it be real if they don't see you cry?

Whether your children are little or grown, seeing you cry allows them to express their emotions as well. Younger children might be frightened at first, but talk to them about how you are feeling to provide them a framework for communicating their feelings. Crying can be perceived as a way of articulating emotions that are difficult to put into words.

Like everything in life—moderation is the key to finding a balance.

Day 210

Add an Ounce of Love to Everything You Do

Go the extra step today by adding love to everything you do:

- Write a note for your child's lunch box.
- Send a handwritten note to a friend.
- Call a loved one and share a wonderful story.
- Bake cookies for a neighbor who has helped you.
- Reach out to a fellow griever with words of encouragement.
- Buy fresh flowers for the dinner table.
- Send an email and attach a fun photo.
- Visit a friend or relative.

Day 211
Kaleidoscope

A kaleidoscope produces a variety of colors, prisms, and other shapes through the use of mirrors that create multiple reflections.

Think of your grief as if you are looking through a kaleidoscope: expressing a variety of reflections through life experiences and memories. Allowing the light to come into your grief (similar to a kaleidoscope) will allow you to see colors and shapes of the people you were so very fortunate to have spent time with before their passing.

Day 212

Heaven: Where Is It?

Wherever you want it to be.

Religious leaders and other individuals have their opinions about where heaven is and what it looks like. In the end, it really is in the eye of the beholder.

Define your own heaven.

Day 213

How Long Will This Last?

The most frequently asked question by grievers is, "How long does the grief journey take?"

For some, the journey is forever, as you will always grieve "what was." However, the extremely emotional part of your journey and the timeline for your immediate grief will mostly occur within the first eighteen months.

Many grievers suffer obstacles when dealing with grief. Depending on a variety of personal circumstances, the journey can become complex. To name a few:

- Your relationship with the deceased
- Complications with the loss—homicide, suicide, accidental death
- Family dynamics
- Financial burdens
- Hardships of the survivors
- Medical complications
- Disability circumstances

For those who are grieving a loss in a more standard environment with fewer hardships, the first year will be filled with the emptiness of shared milestones—birthdays, wedding anniversaries, holiday season, anniversary of the diagnosis, change of seasons, and more. The second year becomes the year to rebuild and recognize the loss has occurred.

For those who are grieving a loss that has complications, the path will be different, as the grievers will be challenged with obstacles preventing them from truly grieving the loss—rather they are "resolving" the complications from the loss.

A general rule of thumb: the first year is the year of exploration, and following the anniversary of the loss the grievers begin to restore their life and find the balance between "what was" and "what is."

Day 214
Memory Box

Talking about personal belongings after the loss of a loved one is an ongoing journey. As the days and months go by following the loss, we have a tendency to revisit the topic frequently. Deciding what to do with the items will evolve over time.

I have created a "Rod box," capturing the essentials of my husband's life. The box might be simple—a large plastic container with a lid—but the contents are filled with intricate items and memories that have no meaning to anyone but me. These include:

- His driver's license
- His passport
- The last phone book with his name in print
- The *Wall Street Journal* from the day he passed
- The shoes our daughter was wearing when we got to the hospital
- Items that were on his desk
- His running log
- His glasses
- His business cards
- A pinecone from where we spread his ashes
- The beer bottle from celebrating his life on top of a mountain
- T-shirts from marathons he ran
- And so much more

When I open the box, I can see him, I can smell him, I can remember so much. And, most important, I can feel close to him.

Day 215

Write Your Own Script

You define your own life—try not to let the loss define you.

Write your script of where you are and where you want to be. Coming up with a game plan and acting on it will help define what is in front of you. Allowing others to do it for you creates a story that is not yours.

Think outside of the box, visualize your potential, and capture it in a manuscript to help you play out your future.

Day 216

Comparing Your Loss to Others'

Be cautious of comparing your loss to others' losses. Often when you lose a loved one, you may look at others who have experienced a similar loss, and you might think they are "in a better place" than you are. Maybe or maybe not.

Although you may have experienced similar losses, the encouragement of your support circle, your family obligations, and the type of death may determine the outcomes of your personal journey. Grievers' outward expressions can often be misread; therefore, what you see may not be what they are experiencing inside.

Day 217

The Physical Experience of Grief

Often we think of grief as an emotional state of being after a loss, as we are overcome by such powerful emotions that it is often impossible to function as we once did. Yet somehow, we do. Unfortunately, we also experience the physical aspects of grief, which occur at the same time—and we have less control over how our bodies react.

For some, the stress associated with the loss can manifest itself in illnesses, inability to function daily, and weight gain or loss. A surprising aspect that we often overlook is the physical reaction to holidays, anniversaries, and birthdays. For example, in anticipation of the anniversary of the loss, your physical body may react. The reaction may occur due to your fear associated with the loss, realization that your loved one has passed, or the anticipation of the anniversary. Regardless of the reason, your body is aware of the dates and responds accordingly. How it happens isn't always obvious, but it just does.

Day 218

Missing the Calls, Emails, and Personal Touches

As months pass by after the loss and you begin settling back into a routine, often what you miss most are the phone calls, emails, text messages, and personal touches that you were so accustomed to receiving from your loved one: the simple love taps in both directions that meant so much on a daily basis.

There is no replacement for the role your loved one played in your life; remaining connected to each other on a daily basis was part of the relationship. With the changes that have occurred since the loss, a void has been created by the lack of phone calls, emails, and text messages. While there is no substitute for the person you have lost, there is an opportunity to build new connections with others based on different aspects of your day. It might have to be more than one person you reach out to in order to feel connected and fill the void left by your loved one.

Day 219

No Reason to Defend Yourself

Don't defend yourself—be proud of your journey and how far you have come. Don't apologize for crying, for talking about your loved one, or for not picking up your house—these things should only matter to you.

Day 220
Try to Avoid the What Ifs

Playing the tapes over and over again in our head: What if our loved one was still with us, how would our lives be different? Would we live in the same house? Would our kids have grown up differently? Would we celebrate holidays with similar traditions?

No matter how we answer these questions the outcome will remain the same—they are only what ifs, as our loved one has passed away. Sometimes it is soothing to pretend and savor the what ifs to feel close to those we lost; therefore, enjoy those moments while reflecting on a life that once was, but be cautious not to remain there for too long.

Day 221

Create a New Tradition

As part of your new way of life, creating a fresh tradition within different aspects of your life will allow you to look forward to special events. Whether the occasion is celebrating your loved one's birthday, enjoying the holiday season, or taking a vacation, breaking the mold of "what was" and adding a spark with a new ritual or routine will provide excitement and pleasure. A few ideas:

- Travel for the holidays rather than staying home—visit a dear friend or relative.
- Throw a birthday party inviting all your loved one's friends—make it an annual celebration to remain connected.
- Rent a beach house for your family for a summer holiday.
- Host a "working" Thanksgiving dinner, where all your guests participate in the preparation of the feast.
- Plan a family reunion.

Day 222
Let in the Light

There is something so magical about light—the incredible feeling of being surrounded by brightness and luminosity, of feeling a glow and a sense of being carefree. Only you can determine when the right time is to feel the radiance of a new day and how to let in the light again.

Day 223

Avoid People Who Are Critical and Try to Steal Your Grief from You

Your friends and family members, as well as coworkers and neighbors, may appear to be critical of your choices while grieving—they only want the best for you. Their actions and words can be interpreted as unfavorable, conveying the desire for you to move on. Don't let them steal your grief from you.

Live each day reminiscing with your loved ones' presence: capture the smells, hear their voices, and feel them in your heart. Do not rush the process, as each phase of grief provides you with a connection to your loss and an opportunity to grow.

Remember, "your people" only want you to feel better and often do not know how to go about helping you. The time will come when you are able to put both feet on the ground and walk through the journey with pride, understanding, and a new connection to your surroundings. Continue to share your journey with "your people," allowing them to further understand you, your loss, and your commitment to find balance.

Day 224

Finding an Outlet
for Creating Something New

Finding a smidgen of daily diversion might be all you
need to find the perfect balance of blending old with new.
Discovering a new outlet to help channel your emotions
and energy will provide a break from your daily thoughts
when needed.

Join a new organization for pleasure or to lend a
helping hand. A few examples include:

- Religious group
- Nonprofit board
- Cultural museum or arts organization
- Book club
- Volunteer organization
- Tennis group
- Game club
- Walking group
- Photography group

All of these will help you get reengaged while being
with others and learning something new. The beauty of
creating something fresh is that you are in control of how
much you share with others regarding your loss, so the
activity can become an oasis.

Day 225

Today's Agenda

Call a family member or friend to see how the person is • Take a walk in your neighborhood or local park • Visit the library to check out a book or DVD • Go to the grocery store and buy yourself a scrumptious treat • Arrange fresh flowers for your house • Serve a meal at a soup kitchen • Attend a matinee movie • Play hooky from work or school • Wash and vacuum your car • Attend a cultural event • Sit on a bench and people watch • Take a drive to a new section of town • Take a bubble bath • Try a new recipe • Provide a random act of kindness for someone • Volunteer your day providing support for a charity • Hug someone special

Start planning tomorrow!

Day 226
Continue to Focus on Life

As the days turn to weeks, and the weeks turn to months since your loss, you will begin to turn the corner of the devastation, finding the will and desire to continue living again. By placing the focus on life you will find happiness, satisfaction, and comfort in knowing you are grieving because you loved someone and you were loved back.

Time has passed, removing the jabbing pain that occurred on a daily basis immediately after the loss. While still painful, the sharpness of the grief becomes slightly more tolerable, allowing you to begin to see the light emerging from the end of the tunnel. As you exit the tunnel, you will find a juncture you have been looking for since the loss—the feeling that you will be okay, and it is now time to focus on what is in front of you, what is important, and what you can control.

Day 227

Find Your Voice

When I lost my husband many years ago, I found myself looking for answers to all my questions: Why did I become a widow? Why did my husband pass away at such a young age? Why was my life chosen as the one to be turned upside down? Those were only a few.

My sadness pulled me inward where I found myself so miserable that I was lost for words—tears flowed easily, but I could not speak. I found myself getting angry at who I became as a result of losing my husband, and I could not find a way to ask for help or find my voice. Getting mad at myself actually made me stronger—I could no longer blame anyone else for the situation I was in and had to dig deeper to find my voice and talk about what I was feeling and what I needed. Once I began talking, the rest began to flow.

Find your words, use them, and let your voice be heard.

Day 228

When You Don't Know What to Do

Wait until tomorrow to answer the question.

The best advice is not to react—hold on as long as you can before making any decisions. You have heard that before. Wait to resolve even the trivial decisions—linger until the answer comes to you in a more logical and informed way.

Once you make a decision, live with what you have decided. No regrets, whether it was the right or wrong decision.

Whether the question is to accept a social invitation, buy a new car, quit your job, ask for help, or move back to your home state, try not to react too quickly by making a rash decision.

Day 229

Creating Goals with Milestones

Every year, regardless of our grieving, we set goals for ourselves that can become very overwhelming, as achieving them often becomes stressful and impossible. When defining goals with milestones, the goals are broken down into smaller achievable pieces, reducing the overwhelming feeling of not being able to accomplish the entire goal and allowing us to feel successes along the way.

A *goal* is the result or achievement toward which effort is directed, and a *milestone* is a significant task related to achieving the goal.

Why Should We Set Goals?

- Get "unstuck"
- Work toward something
- Light at end of the tunnel
- Encouragement
- Change of pace
- Meet new people
- Discover new things
- Reach out of comfort zone
- Be challenged

What Are Milestones as They Relate to Goals?

- Measurable piece of the goal
- Tool to keep interest and momentum
- Sense of accomplishment
- List of needed tasks
- Something attainable

Examples of Goals:

- Take care of yourself (eat right, exercise, hygiene, sleep through the night, wear makeup again, buy new clothes)
- House projects (paint, rearrange furniture)
- Relationships (friends, in-laws, neighbors, dates)
- Children (participate in activities, volunteer at school, improve relationships)
- Move toward finding peace and acceptance (clean out closet, change name on personal accounts, take a vacation, get out of the house more)
- Emotional goals (build a memorial, keep a journal, write letters)
- New adventures (plan a new vacation, ride in a hot-air balloon, attend an opera or play, meet new people, sign up for an athletic event)
- Pamper goals (dress in a cute outfit, cook a new recipe, start an afternoon movie club, take a class)

Day 230
Spending Time Alone

If you find yourself being alone for more than two-thirds of a day, perhaps you should do your best to make a change. While spending time alone is an important aspect of grief, it can also create anxiety. Too much time spent thinking in solitude without enough human interaction and then fused with grief can be a lethal combination.

Try to reduce your time alone, even if you decrease it by just one hour a day.

Day 231
Time Stops

One of my sisters described the first year after my mother's passing as time stopping. She described it as surreal—going through the motions of life: work, family, taking care of her home, and engaging with others, yet not remembering yesterday from last week or last month. While taking care of life essentials, everything else stopped—or at least it appeared to stop.

In my experience, time continued for everyone else around me except for my family, who was mourning the loss. I felt that the second hand on the clock ticked along; however, the sadness of the loss, the emptiness of missing Mom, and the rebuilding of our family without Mom stopped. The standstill caused us to be paralyzed; we lost the ability to muster the strength to lead the way without Mom.

The solution in our hearts was to turn off the clock— savoring our time with Mom for as long as we could, and when the time was right we turned the clock back on. Thanks, Mom, for giving us a much needed break.

Day 232

Hope Does Matter

In life, when we experience a setback from a loss, we often look for the slightest indicator that life without our loved one will be okay, even when we cannot imagine it to be true.

As you travel through your grief journey in the first year, believing in your heart that hope does matter and remaining on course to find hope that you will be okay is all that anyone can ask.

Day 233
Sing

Sing a song—in the shower, walking around your house, driving in your car, walking around the block, or sitting at your desk at work. Who cares whether you have a good voice? Let the music and the lyrics absorb your thoughts and emotions.

Day 234

Surround Yourself with Upbeat People

It might be the time in your journey to spend less time with Eeyore and more time with Winnie the Pooh. Surround yourself with upbeat people who will help you find joy in the little things in life and share a jar half-full of honey.

Day 235

Open an Old Door

Reach deep in your address book for the person you have not seen or spoken to in a while. Find that special person who influenced you in school, in your neighborhood, at work, or as a family member. This is someone you shared a connection with, but the direction of your lives might have placed physical distance between you.

Exchange stories and reconnect as if it had been a century ago since you were together. Take time to realize that the people who were most influential in guiding you are still there for you. The people you have bonded with in the past are most likely the people who know what you need the most.

Day 236
Grief Triggers

Grief triggers often surface at different times and in different ways.

For some, positive triggers can occur from smelling the aroma of bread baking at a bakery while walking down the street, reminding you of the days you baked with your grandmother and triggering memories of warmth and happiness. For others, a particular scene in a movie may cause an emotional reaction of being envious, resulting in a negative trigger.

Most people will experience positive and negative triggers of grief as they are exposed to reminders of the person they have lost. Triggers can be activated by visual experiences, smells, sounds, and occasions. As time goes by, experiencing grief triggers permits you to remain close to your loved ones, constantly letting you know they are still in your life.

Day 237
Prolonged Grief and Loss

Why is it that we think we can avoid grieving if we put it off? Do we really think in our hearts that if we prolong our grief it will go away on its own? Why wouldn't we?

Delaying the realization that your life has taken on new meaning since the loss might sound like a wonderful plan for dealing with the associated pain. But in the end it just doesn't work that way. The death of a loved one creates an emotional and physical reaction that needs attention. Unresolved grief manifests itself in many ways, complicating current and future relationships with family members, friends, and colleagues.

Prolonging grief has a direct correlation to drug and alcohol dependency, mental health issues, and divorce resulting from complications and unresolved emotions caused by the loss.

By addressing your grief immediately you will receive compassionate support from others around you, as they are aware the loss is new. If you prolong your grief, your behaviors may be misinterpreted by others, causing a strain on those around you and creating even greater hardship.

Why make the sadness of the journey last longer than it should?

Day 238

Walking on Ice

A teenager recently shared with me an analogy regarding his grief. He felt as if he were walking on ice, and that the ice would crack, and he would fall into the freezing water below, resulting in drowning because of his sorrow.

He feared his stability, he feared his judgment to step off the ice, and he feared what was next in his life. Walking on ice is a great analogy, as it truly describes the apprehensiveness that occurs during a grief journey—the overwhelming feeling of anxiety associated with the loss, causing irrational fears.

As your journey continues, time will provide strength and logic, allowing you to tame your fear and help you realize when it is time to step off the ice to safety, emerging from the potential threat of the cold water below.

Day 239

Acknowledging Life Has Changed

Grievers are consciously aware on a daily basis that their loss has created a permanent change in their life. There are constant reminders of the void that was left behind following the passing of a loved one, and adjusting to the emptiness becomes a challenge. The longing and missing of a loved one creates a tendency to think the loss did not occur, and life as you once knew it is intact.

Unfortunately, the death will create changes—for many, the changes become a vehicle over time for personal growth; however, at the onset, no griever wants to admit that life has changed. Acknowledging in your heart that your relationship with your loved one has changed and conceding to yourself that daily life, holidays, and future engagements will be different will help create a balance of what was and what is.

Day 240

Grieving Has a Path That Has Its Own Wisdom

As you navigate your path along the way, you will gain strength and knowledge of life, offering insight into what matters each day. Whether your path is paved or a dirt trail, you will find bumps, detours, and roadblocks that will help you steer your emotions using good judgment. Follow the route that is appropriate for you, and don't get alarmed by taking a wrong turn as you absorb your newly found wisdom.

Day 241

Putting Your Own Grief Aside

When a family is grieving together, there is a tendency for one family member to become the central caregiver, often putting their own his off to the side in order to provide support for others.

The natural inclination is for the stronger parent or the oldest sibling to take charge of the situation and forgo his own mourning by remaining strong, coordinating logistics, and always being present for others. Having the emotional toughness to care for others while you are experiencing your own pain is a gift, but at some point putting yourself first becomes a must.

While it might seem like you are putting your own grief aside while caring for others, knowing that you are helping is a way of working through your grief. Be sure to incorporate "me" time and mourn the loss of your loved one.

Day 242

It's Okay to Be Angry with God

After losing a loved one, many grievers find themselves struggling to resolve where religion, and specifically God, fit into their grief journey. There tends to be conflict when making sense of the loss as it relates to religious beliefs—the grievers are torn between being devoted to their religion while being faithful to their hearts.

There are so many questions, yet very few answers, when mourning a loss: Why has this happened to my family and me? Why, if I have been faithful to my family, community, and congregation, is my family suffering? Whether or not you were a firm believer in God prior to the loss, being angry with God is a natural reaction to the loss.

For this moment, let your anger find its place in your grief and religion. As time passes, begin to reach out to those you are connected to in faith and belief, letting the relationship rebuild at its own pace.

Day 243

Healing the Scars

The loss of a loved one creates wounds that can be so deep in the heart and soul that the mending process often leaves scars. Just as for a cut to the skin, applying the correct amount of tender loving care will determine the magnitude of the scar that will remain forever.

Take care of the wound, and reduce the visual scar that will remain in the future.

Day 244

There Is Power in Numbers

Your journey is personal; however, surrounding yourself with people who can influence and help guide the outcome creates a power in numbers. Increasing your support circle boosts the odds of finding peace with the loss.

Day 245

When Is It Time?

In the months following the loss of your loved one, your surroundings become more visible, and the notion of bringing closure to constant reminders of the loss are more apparent. The timeline will vary from person to person, but often the questions nagging you are simple questions with complex answers. When is it time to . . .

- Take off my wedding ring following the loss of my spouse?
- Move the soccer cleats from the backseat of the car?
- Remove the coat from the hook by the front door?
- Rearrange my child's bedroom?
- Open my spouse's desk drawers?
- Change the voicemail message?
- Clean out the closets?
- Sell the car that has been sitting in the garage?
- Empty our parent's house?

The appropriate timing and answer to these questions will vary from person to person. Try not to get hung up on the process but rather manage the emotions of making the decisions.

Day 246

Volunteer with Meaning

A rewarding way to cope with your grief is to volunteer for an organization that is directly connected to the manner in which your loved one passed away. Help save the next life by supporting the group with your time, money, or expertise. Help spread the word for preventing a disease or avoiding an accident.

Research the organizations in your area and apply your energy around the loss to help create a positive outcome.

Day 247

No Rule Book

Grief does not come with a map or guide of how to maneuver through the ups and downs of the journey. There are no rule books regarding what is right or wrong. Given that no two people grieve the same way, create your own rule book that presides over what is right for you!

Day 248
Mourning

Mourning is the open expression of your thoughts or feelings following the loss of a loved one. As with grief and death, mourning takes into account cultural complexities and behaviors of those who are bereaved.

When someone is in mourning, there is a tendency to follow traditional observations during a set period of time. The griever may wear black clothing or withdraw from social events, marking the immediate time following the loss. Customs will vary and have become more relaxed in current times.

For some cultures, there is a belief that when the mourning period is over, it is time to be over your grief. However, for most cultures today, grief is an ongoing reaction to the loss with no set timeline.

Day 249

Finding Your "New Normal"

What was normal for you prior to your loss has changed. Your typical day might have included a phone call or interaction with the person you recently lost or a casual reminder that he or she is still with you. What was customary is no longer a regular occurrence, and what is perceived to be normal is no longer a part of a routine.

Often grievers speak of finding their "new normal"—in essence redefining what is ordinary and typical as it relates to interactions in daily life. As you define your new normal, you will begin to put pieces together in your grief that were difficult to define in the earlier months of grieving. Finding your "new normal" will allow you to create new boundaries with your loved one while balancing your new life.

Day 250

Cleaning Out the Closets

The timing of cleaning out the deceased loved one's personal belongings truly depends on the individual griever. The process generally begins when you are looking for something, are moving, or have chosen to reuse the space for another purpose.

When you are ready, tackle one area, one drawer, or one room. Try not to take on the entire project in one afternoon, as you will become frustrated. A technique that has been successful among fellow grievers is to start with one item at a time and place it in one of five piles:

1. Give to someone
2. Keep for myself
3. Donate
4. Place in trash
5. Don't know what to do with it but do not want to delay the process

This approach will allow you to keep momentum and jump over hurdles that would otherwise slow down the process. When you feel you are slowing down or becoming overly emotional, it is time to walk away and revisit at another time.

Take your time, savor the memories, and feel good about getting organized.

Day 251
Finding an Anchor

There are so many different forms of anchors. An anchor can hold a boat in place while it is floating in water. An anchor can finish a relay at a track or swim meet. An anchor can be a piece of hardware in a wall to hold a picture in place. An anchor can be mounted in a rock to hold a climber's rope.

In these cases, the anchor is used to secure the location or fasten an object or person. In grief, we discover our anchors based on the people who have cared for and shielded us from additional pain—those who protect and hold us firmly in place as we travel through our journey.

Day 252

Experience a Cultural Outing

Immerse yourself in something exciting, resulting in a learning experience, while associating the experience with your loved one:

- Attend a play.
- Visit a museum.
- Participate in a lecture series.
- Attend a concert.
- Take a religious class.
- Learn about regions of the world.

Day 253
Song Names

A few weeks ago I was creating a new playlist on my iPod, and I discovered a trend: many of the songs I have accumulated over the years have a direct correlation to the loss of my husband. The song titles remind me of the love we shared and my grief associated with his loss. To name a few:

- "My Love"
- "Your Love Is My Drug"
- "Somewhere Only We Know"
- "Don't Stop Believing"
- "So Sweet"
- "To Be Able to Love"
- "Beautiful Soul"
- "I'm Gonna Be Alright"
- "Your Smiling Face"
- "How Sweet It Is"
- "You've Got a Friend"
- "I'll Be There"
- "Bruised"
- "Angel"
- "Hope"
- "Wishing"
- "Listen to Your Heart"

Create your playlist.

Day 254

Each Journey Is Unique

Our natural desire is to compare ourselves to people around us—this behavioral trait stems back to our days in elementary school when we wanted to be just like everyone else. Looking and behaving like our friends at the time was a desired goal.

With grief it is the opposite. Each journey is unique, therefore avoiding the comparison to others is actually a better outcome. It is impossible to know what other grievers are experiencing and the circumstances surrounding their loss.

The intimacy of your special journey is unique to you—even your family members who are mourning the same loss will experience their own journey.

Day 255
Out of Balance

Do you feel out of balance—similar to when one tire on a car is not in balance with the other three, creating unsteadiness and an irregular rhythm?

Grief can act as a counterweight, causing grievers to question stability and their steadiness in many aspects of life. The overwhelming feeling of the loss and the resulting emotional and physical reaction can throw somebody off balance. The balance is not restored overnight; it takes time to find poise and create a sense of balance.

Continue to search for harmony in all aspects of your life, and soon you will find your balance.

Day 256
Words of Wisdom

Life is an opportunity, benefit from it.
Life is beauty, admire it.
Life is a dream, realize it.
Life is a challenge, meet it.
Life is a duty, complete it.
Life is a game, play it.
Life is a promise, fulfill it.
Life is sorrow, overcome it.
Life is a song, sing it.
Life is a struggle, accept it.
Life is a tragedy, confront it.
Life is an adventure, dare it.
Life is luck, make it.
Life is too precious, do not destroy it.
Life is life, fight for it.

—*Mother Teresa*

Day 257
Snowy Day

There is nothing more exciting than a snowy day. An excuse to sit in front of the fire with a book, a cup of tea, and a warm blanket while watching the flakes fall from the sky and landing carefully outside your window.

Pull out your journal and write a few entries about how you are feeling and what you have been spending time thinking about; include a reflection on your loved one.

Day 258

A New Perspective

Spending our days mourning the loss of someone we love is exhausting. At some point along the journey, we realize that life as we once knew it has changed, and with that change comes new relationships and a new outlook. Viewing the death as an unfortunate incident, yet knowing your connection with the deceased has influenced you in a positive way, will help you in developing a new perspective on the situation.

Evaluating what was and what is now will help define your new perspective and allow you to change your heartbreaking point of view regarding the loss.

Day 259

Will You Succeed?

Yes, you will indeed. (Ninety-eight and three-quarters percent guaranteed.)

Doctor Seuss is often known for his witty writing and imaginative characters. Originally praised for making the frustrating process of learning to read more enjoyable for young children, Doctor Seuss is also commended for incorporating lessons on life and morality. *Oh, the Places You'll Go!* is a classic and fitting gift for any graduate, but it can really be a reminder of how to be successful and happy at any stage of life. Among the upbeat and enthusiastic motivation, Doctor Seuss certainly doesn't sugarcoat the fact that life is full of loneliness, disappointment, and personal hardship. As he very simply admits, "Un-slumping yourself is not easily done." And unfortunately, there is no medical prescription for slumping. In all of these cases, it is about your willpower and determination to un-slump yourself and not end up in the Waiting Place . . . for people just waiting.

Visit your local bookstore or library and indulge in a bit of wit from Doctor Seuss.

Day 260
Another Big Realization

No one knows what you are going through unless they have been through it themselves. As much as we are exposed to all kinds of human and personal struggle through books, articles, and movies, hardship is complex and difficult to understand from the outside. Our friends and family try to provide the best support and comfort they can, but it's sometimes hard to accept. While in our hearts we know it's genuine, it's not always the kind of support or advice we're really wanting.

The important thing to remember is that while you're confused, at a loss for words, trying to do your best, so is your support system. Grief is inexplicably awful, and unfortunately everyone has to experience it eventually. Don't be surprised if you receive an apology from a friend or family member if and when he or she experiences grief. And take joy in knowing you will truly be an understanding resource for someone in the future.

Day 261
Metamorphosis

Even though your loved one is no longer physically next to you, you can still have a relationship with him or her. Try to think of your recent change as a metamorphosis and not a loss. Find ways to keep your loved one incorporated in your life. For example, use his or her birthday or another special date as an excuse to get family and friends together. Or if you're looking for someone to talk to about an idea or how you're feeling, your loved one will be the perfect listener.

Day 262
Feng Shui

If it hasn't already, there will come a time when you must address your loved one's belongings. From the griever's point of view, there are generally two ways to deal with this situation. On the one hand, you might not want to touch anything because the thought of cleaning out the closet or throwing away his or her toothbrush is too unbearable. On the other hand, a loved one's belongings or that special chair in the living room that is now empty serves as a constant reminder.

Instead of addressing the issue straight on, why not incorporate some of the ideology behind feng shui? Feng shui is a Chinese belief system using the laws of heaven and earth to orient your surroundings and to bring positive energy flow. In regard to your loved one's belongings, focus on the idea of rearranging instead of cleaning out. Rearrange your living room or reorganize your closet. This will give a new feel to your space without you feeling rushed or guilty for "cleaning out."

Day 263
Your Best Friends

Why is it that friends come and go in our lives, especially when we need them the most?

The answer is simple. In life we probably have very few true friends, and the rest are friends who enter our lives during specific periods of time when we share common interests such as raising kids, volunteering for a nonprofit organization, or being neighbors, coworkers, or tennis partners. As interests shift, so do many of our groups of friends.

When grief enters the friendship picture, some will endure the true test of friendship by remaining your best friends. Others will grow distant and carry on their daily activities and find less and less time to be there for you.

A best friend is someone who will be there for you regardless of the situation—identify your best friends and put your energy where you receive something in return.

Day 264

Unresolved Loss

Often grievers experience untimely deaths of loved ones, leaving unresolved issues, complicating the mourning process.

In such cases of unresolved loss, the griever will no longer have the opportunity to work through old issues or resolve challenges in a relationship, resulting in unfinished business and causing excessive guilt and remorse that complicate the future relationship with the deceased.

When grief remains unresolved, it can also lead to serious health problems and social awkwardness, causing the griever to experience depression, anxiety disorders, and even isolation from friends and family.

Sharing unresolved loss with family, friends, or in a therapy session will allow the griever to work through the difficult situation, while redefining the relationship with the person he or she lost and coming to terms with the reality of the loss.

Day 265
Revisit Journaling

Journaling is a great way to capture your thoughts and emotions, providing an outlet to be alone with your grief while being expressive. One of the best gifts of journaling is that the process provides the grievers with an opportunity to revisit their journey by reading earlier entries, thus allowing them to witness their progress.

If you find yourself having trouble with your journal, here are some helpful hints:

Hint	Action
For every lash-out entry, try to write a positive note.	This allows you to release hostility, yet end with something uplifting.
Read your journal a couple of times a month.	This will exemplify your healing progress: how you are coping with your fears and how much stronger you are getting daily.
Make a list of questions.	Answer the questions each month; see how your answers vary.
Write stories about loved ones.	Include how you met, funny stories, what you liked most about the people, and what made them smile.
Draw pictures	See how your pictures change over time from angry and sad to more uplifting
Find a corner or quiet place to write.	This is your time alone with the deceased—be selfish and close out the world.

In each entry, write about yourself.	Writing about your emotions every day will help rebuild your self-esteem. You will see and feel your progress.
If you are comfortable after some time has passed, share your journal entries with loved ones, children, or friends.	Being able to express yourself orally helps you find peace with your loss.

Day 266

Reinforcing Personal Relationships

A positive result of grief is the reinforcing of personal relationships with family and friends.

As time passes from the date of the loss and personal emotions begin to settle down, grievers begin to recognize how precious life is and how it can end so quickly, creating a special bond with survivors associated with the loss. Acknowledging and appreciating the special people around you reinforces their importance and provides you with a sense of gratitude for what you have.

Reach out to those who are associated with the loss by providing support and offering assistance when needed, and bond with each other in a special and personal way.

Day 267

Recipient of Personal Belongings

As the recipient of a loved one's personal belongings, your relationship with the person will change over the course of the life of the items. As your relationship with the departed evolves, so will your connection with the specific item providing a special bond.

When a surviving sister received clothing items from her sister's husband, at first she was unable to look at the items or consider wearing them. As time has passed, she finds great comfort with the clothing, which provides warmth as she puts it on. A friend was given his running buddy's watch as a memory; he finds great comfort on his runs, knowing that his partner is still running with him.

As you decide what to do with some of the personal items of a loved one, be sure to share the items with others, as it will provide great pleasure knowing that you will provide a lifetime connection to the person that they too have lost.

Day 268

Love Is the Driving Force

On those days when you feel like you are taking a few steps backward in your journey, always remember that "love is the driving force" causing the pain, loneliness, and sorrow. Without the love you would never experience the pain, and that love will help you survive the agony created by the loss.

Day 269
Someplace, Somewhere, Sometime

You will be together again.

Day 270

Agree to Disagree

Mourning the loss of a loved one results in many life lessons along the journey. What once was significant may no longer be important.

What is key is not to fret over things you do not have control over. Specifically, avoid arguing over issues that really don't matter. For example, if a story is being told and some of the facts are out of context or embellished, let it go. In the end, it does not matter who is right or wrong; you are both entitled to an opinion. Agree to disagree and move on to the next topic.

When in doubt, always take the high road.

Day 271

Rebuilding after a Loss

You have recently been derailed by the loss, and it is now time to reinvent your life by rebuilding who you are.

Start by looking in the mirror and answering a few questions:

- Are you taking care of yourself?
- Do you like what you see?
- Do you appear to be happy?
- Are you getting regular sleep?

For any answers that are not a yes, start working on a plan to correct the situation. You have to like what you see in the mirror to start rebuilding your life. Once you complete the first step, move on to bigger areas and ask the next set of questions:

- Are your days filled with love and happiness?
- Have you established a new relationship with your loved one?

Determine the areas in your life that are creating the most stress and correct or eliminate the challenge.

Part of the rebuilding will be restoring, while the rest will be discovering. Either way, reestablishing and renovating you is what is important.

Day 272
Finding Passion Again

Following the loss of someone special, we often lose passion in our lives; the ensuing extreme emotions result in less energy and enthusiasm. By finding something to be passionate about, you will be able to reengage and refocus. Here are some tips to start finding your passion:

- Reflect on who you were before your loss—determine what gave you pleasure in life. Create a list of what excited you—for example, travel, team athletics, volunteering, or spending time with kids.
- Brainstorm a list of ideas that you could become passionate about—an athletic goal, planning a trip, obtaining further education for a career or hobby (master's degree or photography class), working with a charity or nonprofit organization, moving closer to family, or facilitating a grief group.
- Prioritize the list—consider working on two ideas congruently.
- Reflect on the journey.

Find purpose in life again by engaging in something that you are passionate about.

Day 273
Relinquish Control

As grievers, we have a penchant for wanting to be in control. We want to maintain control of our emotions, our surroundings, our next steps, and with whom we want to spend time. We fret the thought of any additional emotions entering our daily routine, so having control will allow us to know exactly what is coming our way. The challenge is that staying in control often creates more stress because having power over our surroundings is virtually impossible.

Try to relax some aspects of your day. Let the cards fall and see where they land.

Day 274
Gifts of Grief

What a strange concept—thinking that one can experience gifts associated with losing a loved one. As surprising as the concept is, the notion is so true.

After losing a loved one, we often spend time introspecting the loss—realizing where our priorities lie, pondering our own mortality, and reflecting on our relationship with the person we lost. The introspection results in becoming closer to our family members, becoming better friends, and becoming better parents.

Learning how to articulate emotions while functioning on a daily basis is often a new reality. For many, there is a belief that the emotional gain from the loss is a gift. Spending more quality time with family and friends is recognized to be a gift, as we have learned from the loss how short and precious our lives are. Taking better care of ourselves after watching a loved one suffer from a terminal illness is a gift.

No loss of life is worth the gifts; however, what we learn from the loss and how we react can become a gift.

Day 275
What Complicated Grief Can "Look" Like

Complicated grief can be defined as grief that is complex and problematic. For some, the harshest parts of their grief are caused by external factors such as unresolved grief, family dynamics, or financial hardships. Others remain "stuck" in their grief, preventing them from healing, finding passion again, or making adjustments in order to become accustomed to the reality of their loss. A few tell-tale signs that someone is experiencing complicated grief:

- The griever has extreme difficulty speaking of the deceased without an emotional reaction.
- The griever has become reclusive and solitary.
- The griever is having difficulty maintaining daily responsibilities, including work, taking care of the home, or interacting with others.
- The griever is making immediate and sudden changes in his or her lifestyle.
- The griever has emotional outbursts caused by minor events.
- The griever has sleeping challenges.
- The griever shows self-destructive behaviors.

If you or any fellow griever is experiencing intense reactions to grief, it might be time to seek professional help.

Day 276
Find the Perfect Grief Location

Search for that perfect place to be alone with your loved one—a place that provides solace and comfort at a time in your life when you need to be calm, soothe your hurt, and ease your pain. Discover the special place just for *you*.

Whether it is sitting by the ocean listening to the waves crash on the shore, climbing a mountain and absorbing the spectacular views, or sitting in your backyard, find your sacred place and connect with the person you have lost.

Day 277
Hope Heals

If only we could place a Band-Aid with a bit of ointment on our pain and wait a day until the cut heals and we recover. Unfortunately, grief is not that simple.

Having optimism that everything is going to be okay, and finding the faith, desire, and wish to know you will be okay is a form of hope. The underlying trust that you will find the strength to adjust to the new circumstances is what your new life is about.

Finding the path to recovery, whether spiritually or emotionally, will provide the healing powers that will enable you to embrace the loss.

By restoring faith that you will be okay and using the strength you have developed through your personal journey, you can prove that hope heals.

Day 278

Life Is a Triangle

Visualize your life as a triangle.

- Birth—love—death
- Body—mind—spirit
- Relaxation—self-care—growth

The relative length of the sides defines a triangle. In an equilateral triangle all the sides are the same, in an isosceles triangle two sides are equal, and in a scalene triangle all sides are unequal.

In your personal triangle, the angles may shift over the years, creating different types of triangles while keeping all sides connected.

Day 279

Expanding Your Horizons

Reach out past your current sphere to find something vastly different from what you are currently participating in.

- Attend a cooking school.
- Experience an archaeological exploration.
- Attend a music festival.
- Take a photography class.
- Learn about art appreciation.
- Trace your family lineage.
- Learn a foreign language.
- Partake in a historical pilgrimage.
- Take a sports class.
- Create a self-improvement program.

Day 280

Being There for Fellow Grievers

So much transpires when you lose a loved one that it often takes months to digest what has happened around you regarding your relationships, survival, and personal growth. As you come up for air, you realize what guided you through your journey, what helped, and what is important to you. This realization will help blaze the trail for the next round of grievers, as you share your knowledge and understanding of the process.

A special message sent to me from one of my sisters is a great example of what is important to a fellow griever:

> I remember when Rod died and I was in college . . . before I flew to the funeral I went to the psychologist at school and asked her what to say to you to make you feel better. . . . I will never forget what she told me . . . she said, "It will never matter what you say to your sister, it will only matter that you were there." I have really embraced that through the loss of Mom. . . . I can't even tell you what people said to me during her illness, at the funeral, or after her death . . . but I can sure tell you who was there for me . . . and that has really been important to me.

Day 281
Saying Yes to Life Again

When you dig deep into your heart and say yes to life again (and really mean it), you will feel the weight fall off of your shoulders and the desire to live and laugh again.

Start by pulling your shoulders back and standing up straight; follow that by taking a huge breath and letting it out with energy and excitement. It is time to get your life back on track as it once was. In life there will always be stressful challenges, untimely deaths, and uncertainties that will challenge our existence and the energy it takes to wake up every day.

There is only one way of getting around the stresses, and that is saying yes to life again and attacking the doubtful and hesitant days with strength and perseverance. Say *yes*!

Day 282
Listen, Listen, Listen

Now that your journey is underway, people around you will offer advice whether you ask for it or not. They will share their opinion of how you should and shouldn't feel, how they have overcome the difficulties associated with loss, and what your future appears to be.

Of course, some of the recommendations will be wonderful, helpful, and inspiring; others might feel intrusive and bold. We know that the people around you are only trying to help, so my suggestion is to listen, listen, and listen. Embrace what you want, ignore what you are not comfortable with, and ponder the rest.

As you take the advice from others, listen carefully and only engage in what is important to you.

Day 283

Are We Resilient?

Yes, we are.

How do I know? I have worked with so many grievers over my years, and I have watched people rebound in wonderful and enduring ways. Just as Rome was not built in a day, your recovery will not happen overnight. What will happen is that you will learn how strong you are, how important your relationships are with friends and family, and mostly that you are capable of overcoming adversity.

As you bounce back to the old you, embrace the new aspects as well.

Day 284
Make Your Own Choices

If you make a choice that others around you disagree with, it is okay—the world will continue, and you will be okay and learn. Make the mistakes—it is a part of the process and journey. Thank those around you for their opinions about selling your house too soon, spending too much money to help you feel better, remarrying before people think you should, or staying home if you need to.

Make your own choices by accepting opinions from others, contemplating their points of view, and then formulating your own perspective on the subject.

Day 285

Sea Glass

Sea glass—often referred to as beach glass—is weathered glass found along sea- and lakeshores. Over time, friction with sand and water smooths away the sharp edges from the glass, resulting in a smooth, frosted surface.

Just like sea glass, grief softens with time.

Day 286

Unfortunate Turn of Events

Recently, I heard a friend of a widow refer to the untimely death of her husband as an unfortunate turn of events. His words represented grief in a very real and precise manner.

As I pondered his description, I reflected on my own loss, which was very unlucky and came at an inopportune time. What I appreciated about his words, which will remain in my heart, is that the turn of events that occurred were unfortunate; however, my connection to my husband will be forever.

Day 287
Finding Your Community

The days, months, and years following the loss of a loved one are taxing. During these times, being mindful of the importance of taking care of ourselves and caring for others around us is what life is about. The most powerful gift we can offer each other is a community where people can interact, share their thoughts, and feel welcome.

Find or create your community.

Day 288

Reconnect Your Inner Compass

A compass is a navigational instrument that provides direction, based on a physical location while pointing north, relative to the surface of the earth.

Similar to the physical compass, each of us carries an inner compass—often known as instinct—that can keep us on track during our grief, providing a source of strength, advice, and passion. As grievers, our intuition is often challenged, preventing us from feeling confident about the path we are on.

Reconnecting to your inner compass will allow your instinct to make the right decisions, to set priorities, and to determine what is best for you—and most important, to provide the direction to keep you on track.

Day 289

I Remember

- Holding your hand
- Feeling your touch
- Walking barefoot on the beach
- Seeing your beautiful smile
- Sharing birthday wishes
- Enjoying laughter
- Watching glowing sunsets
- Accepting your care
- Receiving strength from your presence
- Having your guidance
- You

Day 290
When Does Grief End?

When you realize you really can live again. But does it actually end, or do you find a way to live with the grief?

Day 291

Finding Your Spirituality

There is something about a loss that compels the survivors to search further into the meaning of life, often starting with their own spirituality. As grievers search for the meaning of life, they spend time discovering the essence of their own beings.

Finding your spirituality is often compared to finding meaning in your life, offering inspiration and connection. For some, it is by way of spiritual practices that can include prayer, meditation, and religious beliefs. For others, having a spiritual experience through the loss, through the divine realm, or through nature can help connect an individual to the deceased.

Spirituality is very personal, comes in many forms, and is what relates to and affects an individual's human spirit.

Day 292

Keep Some Traditions, but Create New Ones as Well

The blending of old and new traditions is the key to finding balance in all aspects of life following a loss.

Capturing traditions and passing them down to future generations allows the grieving family to feel as though their loved one will always be a part of the customs and rituals associated with their family. After the loss, it is important to add new traditions surrounding holidays, birthdays, important celebrations, and life milestones. By creating new experiences, the next generation takes part in establishing the family's traditions.

Combining the old and the new creates a balance of remembrance, tribute, and opportunity.

Day 293

Reserve the Right to Change Your Mind

Through you journey you have earned the right to be you. Now it is time to exercise your right and change your mind if that is what you need to do.

- If you accepted an invitation to a dinner and you no longer want to go, inform the host.
- If you implied you would never be in a relationship again after being widowed and then decide you do not want to be alone, go on a date.
- If you suggested you could help a neighbor who was grieving and you don't feel you have the strength, opt out of helping.
- If you are working on a strict budget and today you want to indulge, go for it.

Some days you just need to change your mind.

Day 294

Feel the Love

The happiness you feel in your heart is often in direct proportion to the love you give. Give love and you will receive love.

Day 295

Each New Day Brings New Strength and New Thoughts

Focusing on a chance for a new beginning each day can change a griever's perspective significantly. In other words, try to let go of old thoughts or habits that may be keeping you from getting where you want to go. We all have these habits—conditioned ways of thinking and acting—that may not work for us any more given the loss we've experienced. A habit is simply something you're not aware you're doing. When you're aware of what you're doing, the action then becomes a conscious choice. By letting go of old habits and being willing to make the choice to move in a different direction, you open yourself up to life supporting you more fully in the ways it can best do so.

Day 296
It's Okay to Be Sad

There are no right or wrong ways of expressing how you feel, so it is okay to be sad. While we strive not to be sad all the time, having bad days is absolutely appropriate and very acceptable.

Taking the appropriate time to reflect is essential. As you define your new relationship with your loved ones, look into the future and learn how to live without their physical presence, adjusting to those emotions that are often uncontrollable. Take the time you need to reflect and rebound as you see fit.

Day 297
Official Language of Grief

There are words and phrases associated with grief that are hard to understand unless you have experienced a loss. The jargon of a griever has its own beat—a combination of sharing, listening, helping, hurting, building, repairing, and living.

What is the official language of grief? A special kind of vocabulary that takes place with words, thoughts, gestures, and expressions, allowing people to communicate with one another on an emotional level.

Day 298

Grief Can Be a Roller Coaster

The feelings you experience during your grief journey can best be described as being on a roller coaster that is full of ups and downs, highs and lows, and the feeling of not being in control.

With grief you can get a burst of highs similar to climbing into the roller coaster car at the beginning of the ride, and a burst of lows like the feeling in your stomach as you descend a steep grade. Comparable to grief, the burst can show up in the middle of the ride—just when you think you are okay, there will be another dip sending you into an emotional tizzy.

Unlike a ride at the amusement park, however, grief is not over in five minutes. Your ups and downs and highs and lows continue, but how you react to those changes will determine when the ride is over.

Day 299
Acknowledge Your Loss

You might feel as though you have acknowledged your loss by taking care of necessary logistical and ceremonial tasks. You have changed names on legal documents, cleaned out drawers and closets, and even worked on a plan for the future. All these tasks are important to get to the next step in grieving.

As grievers, we can often go through the task list and complete the "mandatory" pieces of acknowledging the loss, but the piece we avoid is the emotional acknowledgment. Logically we know that our loved ones have passed; however, emotionally we believe they are still with us. The best way to acknowledge the loss emotionally is by redefining your relationship with your loved one. If you accept in your heart that the relationship now has a different meaning, a different kind of dependency, and a different significance, you will spend emotional thoughts creating that relationship and acknowledge the loss has occurred.

Day 300

What Drives You through Your Grief?

What drives me:

- Remaining connected to my loved one
- Holding on to his memory and feeling his presence
- Keeping his spirit alive
- Surrounding myself with his family
- Capturing the memories we shared
- Looking in the eyes of my daughter and seeing him, knowing the apple does not fall far from the tree

Day 301

Playing the Hand You Were Dealt

There are many analogies that relate grief directly to playing cards. Just like being dealt a hand in any card game, there are many variables—some chance, some fate, and some fortune. There is also some misfortune and hard luck. With that hand, our actions, strategies, and perseverance might provide a winning outcome. We have choices, and how we exercise those options makes the difference.Most important, how we react to the winning and losing based on variables that are out of our control will make all the difference in the outcome. There are wild cards that are dealt, and when you receive one, use it wisely, strategically, and with care.

Day 302

Mourning Lost Promise

Listening recently to a media report on a tragic event, the news reporter shared her interpretation of the deaths, as a community mourned the lost promise of each of these young and vibrant people.

These words resonated, as the explanation was so truthful. No matter how old, no matter how talented, no matter what the circumstance, the untimely death of a loved one leaves a future void in all our lives. In addition to grieving the loss, we grieve the potential that the person will never have the opportunity to reach.

Day 303

Fog Starts to Lift

Looking over a harbor in the morning, you may find the sun's rays struggling to shine through the early morning fog—a beautiful sight, as the mass of sailboats peeks through the mist. You wonder if the sun will shine today, and in most cases it always does.

Just as in grief, you may often feel as though you are hiding in a cloud, and if the cloud went away maybe the sun would shine through and the rays would give you a boost for the day, which you desperately need. Just as in nature, the fog will lift—maybe not as fast and scientifically, but it will, and the beam of light will provide the strength and encouragement that you need.

Day 304
Missed Events

Your loved one will miss all future life events, triggering the survivors to further ache for their loved one. Some of the most frequently asked questions include:

"Who will walk down the aisle with me when I get married, as my father has passed?" For some, another male family member will fill the void, for others, creating a new and less traditional approach, such as walking down the aisle with your mother, a sibling (or multiple), your pet, or by yourself, carrying a memento of your father.

"How do I include my loved one in special birthdays and events?" If you feel comfortable (based on the attendees), create a cutout or bring a picture in a frame of your loved one and be sure to set a place at the table. If this is inappropriate for the event, be sure to toast or recognize your loved one.

"How do I include my mother in my graduation?" Wear an article of her clothing or a piece of jewelry to feel her presence. Look through her graduating yearbook and savor the resemblance of how much you look like each other. Reach out to one of her friends to hear stories about what she was like at your age.

Day 308

Turning Pain into Power

Use the pain you have endured from your loss and turn it into power, helping those around you. When you help others, you are really helping yourself.

Apply the knowledge gained from the sorrow you have felt, the anxiety it has caused, and the emotional distress it has created. This can be accomplished by supporting an organization associated with the type of loss you experienced. If the death was a form of cancer, get involved with finding a cure. If it was a meaningless accident, find a way to create safe measures that will help ensure the misfortune does not happen again. If it was just an unfortunate situation, help the next round of grievers by sharing your knowledge.

As we know in other aspects of our lives, pain can create strength and give you the influence to do something great. Reach out and empower yourself to use your agony in a positive and productive manner.

Day 309

Learn to Walk before You Run

Grief, as with everything else in life, takes time to adjust to and master. Fundamentally, grief is difficult for everyone. And there is no one way to grieve. A great deal of emphasis is put on the stages of grief; however, grievers experience many different characteristics in any number of combinations. What's important here is to first and foremost understand that grief will impact you physically, emotionally, mentally, and spiritually, and it will change as you move through your first year of grief.

As your journey continues, embrace each of these changes in a thoughtful and meaningful fashion, and you will notice your stride getting longer, eventually turning into a run.

Day 310

Big Decisions

It might be time to start thinking about those big decisions that have been hovering over you through the first year of your loss. You have been counseled not to embrace the process and to put aside the decision making until you become more logical and less emotional.

The best way to start the process is to identify the big decisions that are dominating your thoughts—whether they are financial, emotional, or logistical. Once you have identified the challenges, brainstorm the options available, regardless of whether they are fully feasible or not. For each option you have identified, write pros and cons of how it can work. For example, if moving to your home state to be closer to family is your big decision, write the pros and cons of moving, including financials, friends, schools, support circle, and weather.

The pros and cons will allow you to think more logically and less emotionally. Share your findings socially with friends and family to help guide you to a meaningful conclusion. Take your time, and avoid making a hasty decision.

Day 311

Where Are My Friends?

As you begin to come up over the clouds that surround you and feel a bit more social, you begin to find the next challenges. These include your circle of friends.

Whether or not we experience a loss in life, our friends shift based on age group, children, hobbies at the time, health, work, and so many other influences. For many, a death creates a shift as well. If you recently became widowed, socializing as a couple is awkward; if you lost a child, it is often difficult to attend a neighborhood barbecue. Each shift will bring in a new group of friends who have similar interests.

Try not to dwell on those friends you lost; rather, embrace the new ones and build those relationships. Your old friends are still there for you, and over time, you can redefine your relationships with them as you begin to feel more comfortable.

Day 312

Winter, Spring, Summer, or Fall

Our life going forward demands an ever-changing climate, various seasons where our thoughts and emotions are tailor-made to the circumstance in which we find ourselves. Every season has a time of beauty, and how that beauty manifests itself in you measures your progress through your journey.

Day 313

Spend the Day Outside

Turn off your computer and television and head out
the door.

Plan a day to get out of the house, breathe the air, and
take in your surroundings. If it is sunny, grab a hat and
sunscreen; if it is raining, put on waterproof shoes and find
an umbrella; and if it is snowing, grab a coat and scarf.

People have a tendency to be more creative, happier,
and better able to focus when they experience the outdoors.

Day 314
Does Time Heal Wounds?

By now you are wondering what the healing process really feels like. The "new normal" has set in, and while you continue to have emotional strains on your heart, you have begun to march to the beat of a different drummer. Does this mean that time has healed your wounds?

Personally, I believe that your wounds will always be there, but what time has provided is an opportunity for you to redefine the pain. The lost opportunity with your loved one will continue to tug at your heart, leaving a void. However, the healing process will provide you with coping tools to put the change in perspective.

Day 315

Maintaining Family Relationships

For some families, the loss of a loved one triggers an outpouring of love and support. For other families, the loss creates tension, hurt, and loss of direction. Death can bring out the best and worst in all of us, and rekindling those relationships that have been tested through emotions will add so much richness to life. Maintain and rebuild relationships by understanding:

- No two people grieve alike.
- Family members have different coping capabilities.
- People communicate differently.
- Folks have different priorities.
- Relatives have various pulls on their time and emotions.

Mostly—remain positive, assume the best in people, and try not to judge their actions.

Day 316

Step Out of Your Comfort Zone

Reach out of your emotional and physical surroundings—
that area of discomfort and unknown. Challenge yourself
to overcome the anxiety associated with the first step, and
embrace the newness as well as excitement of something
fresh and challenging.

Best of luck.

Day 317

Adjusting to Life without Your Loved One

Life is a continual adjustment. We adjust to the changes in weather, the growth of our children, our aging parents, our overgrown landscaping, our new neighbors, our physician's retirement, and so much more. However, adjusting to life without your special loved one is much more challenging. Finding the balance between the absence, your emotions, and your will to proceed often conflict as you adjust to your new life. Think of the change as a continual process that will be further fine-tuned as time goes on. Try not to modify all aspects of your life at once; rather, alter and rework as your journey continues.

Day 318
Finding Joy

Sadness, disappointment, and severe challenges are events in life, not life itself. These hardships often test our feelings of joy and happiness, as they are overwhelming and result in a griever questioning life in general. For many, grief becomes the confining center of everything we do, and breaking that pattern is difficult and scary. At some point, all grievers need to take the plunge and look for joy.

Start by asking yourself a few questions: Do you take time each day to discover how beautiful your life can be? How long has it been since you watched the sunset? When did you last stare into the night sky, letting the twinkling stars ignite your imagination?

Your joy in life depends on enriching your relationship with your surroundings and with others. Try not to concentrate on what you don't have or have lost. Simple, rejuvenating experiences surround us. They can be safety valves to keep tensions down and spirits up.

Day 319

How Do You Make Sense of the Challenging Things That Happen in Your Life?

We are not born with all the wisdom we need; it comes with growth and maturity. We also will not have all the answers to our questions; many will remain a mystery. And why some people endure life challenges while others experience none will also be a lifetime question that may not be answered.

In order to make sense of the challenges you have endured, accept them by challenging yourself to cope. You can spend your entire life looking for answers or comparing your hardships to others; however, that will result in resentment and becoming unproductive. Spend your energy on working through the challenge rather than making sense of it.

Day 320

Paying It Forward by Helping the Next Round of Grievers

You are so much stronger, wiser, and experienced than the new set of grievers. At times you may feel the complete opposite, but if you were to sit down with a recent griever you would offer expertise, advice, and mostly provide hope that he or she will be okay.

Looking back to your early days of grief, the people who you felt most comfortable with were those who "understood" what you were going through—the people you connected with because of your loss or a loss they had experienced.

Reach out to the next round of grievers and provide wisdom, support, and a much-needed hug.

Day 321
Grief Debate

A debate is a method of arguing, typically about issues of public interest, where persuasive arguments are presented for consideration. Debates usually take place in public, but in this case, why not make it personal?

In the case of your grief, debating it might become a tool for pondering where you are and where you are going. You can deliberate on what is essential, contemplate what is next, and consider all the aspects of your grief. While this might not sound productive, it is simply another tool to help with your reflection on grief.

Day 322
One Day It Changes

One day you wake up and the grief is not as heavy. How this happens and when it happens is a mystery to many of us.

Not sure how or why—it just does. You begin feeling like yourself again. You become enthused about aspects of your life and begin to reengage with meaning.

It is not an overnight process—but it does happen.

Day 323
New Outlook on Life

Today, let's plan to start with a new viewpoint of what is in front of us:

- Create a positive attitude toward people.
- Change your viewpoint on areas of constant worry.
- Take a stance on what is important, but let the rest roll off your shoulders.
- Use a constructive approach to solving challenges.
- Remain optimistic.
- Encourage pleasant behavior from those around you.

Start with today, and then carry over your accomplishments.

Day 324
Gift of Experience

Experience provides clarity—transparency of thought, expression, and feeling. Those things will continue to help you along the way and blaze a path to guide you.

Along with your experiences, you have inherited gifts. The pain and suffering you have endured from the loss have provided strength and understanding, transformed priorities, created new friendships, renewed family relations, and so much more. Capture the gifts you have received from your experiences by cherishing what you have learned, helping others through your wisdom, and feeling good about how far you have come.

Day 325

Do Something on Your Loved One's Bucket List

Sounds crazy, but do it anyway.

As part of my recovery, I took on the wild idea that I would pursue my husband's desire to compete in the Hawaiian Ironman Triathlon. I thought it would be a great tribute and dedication to a man who was unable to obtain one of his own personal goals before his untimely death. Although it was a crazy idea, I was able to cross it off his bucket list.

Choose something as extreme as I did or a bit less complicated. You will be pleasantly surprised how rewarding and fulfilling the idea is when you can check it off.

Day 326
Life

Simple words that illustrate a complex concept:

- Existence
- Days
- Survival
- Way of living
- Continuation
- Being
- Reality
- Ongoing

Define your life.

Day 327

Learning from the Ones
We Have Lost

A lesson from someone who lost her mom when she was thirty-five:

> I don't think I realized what it really takes to be a mother. Although at times my mom drove me crazy, and I didn't always understand her or agree with her, I respect her so much more now that I have lost her (and that is difficult to realize after you have lost someone). . . . It takes a lot of effort to be a mom, and I realized it after she was gone. . . . My biggest "aha" moment from this realization is to tell people to appreciate what they have before it is gone.

Moms have a tendency to continue teaching us even after they are gone. The loss can be a great learning tool to guide you through your future.

Day 328

Twists and Turns

The road of grief has many twists and turns. Around each corner there is another street, intersection, and crossroad, asking a griever to contemplate how to find the final destination, which is looming in the distance.

Just like the road we are traveling on, our moods and relationships take these unexpected twists and turns—sometimes through sheer happenstance, sometimes through calculated decisions. In the end, it is about learning from the journey and worrying less about the final destination.

Day 329

Bridge the Gap

There will always be obstacles to bridging the gap between your life before the loss and your current grief journey.

Newly bereaved are encouraged to press on and show commitment to working through the many ups and downs that are experienced after a loss. As time passes, the expectations increase that the grieving process should come to an end. In reality, there is no end—the before and after are connected by the bridge.

Each day, strive to bridge the gap, which exists between where you are now and the goal you intend to reach.

Day 330
Holding It Together

Why can grievers hold it together better than anyone else? Because the worst thing that could happen already has.

Individually you may feel as if you are living in chaos, confusion, and disorder, but you are actually functioning while under the worst emotional distress. Not only are you functioning, you are helping others, maintaining daily activities, and learning so much about the strength you have within.

Keep the positive outlook, maintain the integrity, and show the world that you are "holding it together."

Day 331

"You Are Not Alone"

Soaring Spirits Loss Foundation created a program titled You Are Not Alone, which has proven to be a lifesaver for those who are widowed. Realizing that you are not alone in your grief and feeling the strength of others around you is what carries grievers through the journey.

Whether you are widowed, have lost a child, or are experiencing an anticipatory loss of a loved one, knowing you are not alone will provide the strength to make it through each day. Reach out to those who have had a similar loss.

Day 332

Circuit Breaker

Do you ever wish that, like a circuit breaker at your house, the switch in your brain would shut off when overloaded? Just imagine how you would be able to relax and put grief to the side—even if it was for a short time.

Although our brains don't have circuit breakers per se, if the demands on you are more than it can meet, your body "blows a fuse." The resulting fatigue forces you to use less energy, protecting you from harm. Although a circuit breaker may protect the circuitry in the home, it does little good if you do not know how to turn it back on or that it even exists. For each griever that switch will be different; therefore, try resetting your circuit breaker based on your current needs.

Day 333

Anniversary of Your Loss

The anticipation of the anniversary is much worse than the actual day. This is primarily due to remembering where you were last year at this time and realizing that a year has already gone by since your loss.

Plan something special for the day. What that looks like will depend on what you are in the mood for. Some grievers would rather be alone, while others would prefer to surround themselves with people who are associated with the person they lost.

Regardless of who you spend the day with and what you choose to do, make the day special by embracing the time with your loved one.

Day 334
Angeliversary

When referring to the pending anniversary of your loved one, it is often hard to describe what you are really recognizing or celebrating on that day. The date references the anniversary of the loss, but how should you reference the date with others? Many grievers just describe the day as the anniversary of the loss. Others reference it as the "deathiversary." A dear friend referenced her loss and day of celebration as an "angeliversary." After all, isn't the person you lost an angel?

Day 335

Second Year: What to Expect

The second year after the loss provides a bit more stability. A griever has already experienced the "firsts" of a calendar year, including birthdays, anniversary, and diagnosis of the illness, as well experiencing graduations, weddings, and other life events.

For some, the second year proves to be much more tolerable, as the anticipation of the unknowns has passed and the grievers are less emotional. The grievers are more aware of how they will react to certain situations and have their expectations more intact. For others, the second year is more stressful, as the grievers limped through the first year and now feel as if they have to face the reality of their loss.

The majority of grievers will find a balance between these extremes, with the hope of finding happiness and adjusting to their new lives.

Day 336

Measuring What Is Important

It's essential that you measure your daily progress by determining what's most important to you, which is having the courage to follow your heart and intuition and not what others think is best for you.

Day 337
Stop Planning

For today, this week, and even this month, leave space in your calendar without appointments, engagements, or scheduled outings. Take the time to relax and enjoy the moment. Go with the flow, whether it is "nesting" in your home or reading a book.

In the earlier days of grief, a coping mechanism was to create a plan and execute it to help settle the emotions of the loss while engaging in activity. As time passes, switching gears to less scheduled activities will allow you to relax more while feeling more comfortable.

Day 338

Reflecting on the Year

Take the time to reflect on the year that has passed. Pull out your journal, find a box of tissues, and pour a cup of tea or glass of wine. As you flip through the pages, you will be able to see the progress you have made with your emotions, your ability to think more clearly, and the new relationship that has developed with your loved one.

Even if you have not physically written your thoughts in a journal, they have been captured in your heart. Close your eyes and reflect on the first couple of days after your loss and note where you are today. You have come a long way—there will always be good and bad days, but the year has proven that the pain of grief will subside, even if it's in small quantities.

Day 339
Your Map

It might be time to create your personal map by plotting directions, routes, and attractions. The beauty of creating a map is that you can devise a strategy and execute the plan while maintaining the flexibility to take an alternate path to get to your final destination.

Day 340

Changes You Forever

Grief can transform a human forever. The experience of losing someone you love, the permanency of the loss, and the emotional reaction leave an everlasting impression on relationships, activities, and the future.

For most, the changes are positive. People who have experienced a loss have a tendency to love a little deeper as they move forward, have a bit more patience for those who are suffering, and appreciate what they have, as tomorrow it may be gone.

Day 341

Do You Ever Get "Over It"?

No, and why should you?

Cherish the memories, savor the moments, and reminiscence about a wonderful life that was shared.

Day 342

Write Your Story

Everyone has a story to tell, and yours is just as compelling as the others. Your experiences, your emotions, and your outcomes are worthy of documenting, whether verbally or on paper—and they should be shared.

Start by writing notes, then organize the notes and write away. Be sure to capture life-changing events—how you felt about them and the outcomes. Include thoughts of growth and disappointment—what went right and what went wrong.

When you are ready, share the story with friends, family, and even new acquaintances. You will be pleasantly surprised by the reaction of others, as they will listen attentively with both ears.

Day 343

Learn from Yesterday; Live for Today; Hope for Tomorrow

You learned from your early days of grief what yesterday represents. Now spend each day with an attitude of reflection and improvement. Our attitude has a profound effect on the quality of our life each day. Therefore, find a few minutes each morning to clear your mind and think positive thoughts about the upcoming day. Focus on the people and events that have supported you through your grief journey, and then take some time to look forward to everything you want to accomplish. Now carry that feeling with you all day long, even during the less enjoyable activities. Let your optimism flow into your hope for tomorrow.

Day 344
Rain

There is something about rain that is soothing. The combination of moisture in the air, the smell of the rainwater as it touches the ground, and the tapping of the raindrops on the windows that provide a warm feeling.

Just like grief, there are many dimensions of a rainstorm that can come and go in one weather pattern. Each period of wet weather can be labeled as a drizzle, downpour, shower, or even a hurricane. With each storm, the sun returns and the ground dries, making for a new day.

Day 345

Do Something Crazy Today

- Go to a matinee movie—buy popcorn and even stay for a double feature.
- Go skydiving and jump out of an airplane.
- Eat breakfast for dinner.
- Go back to your high school and watch a sporting event.
- Paint a room in your house.
- Play hooky from work or school.
- Walk or ride your bicycle to work.
- Try a new activity.

In summary, drop the routine today.

Day 346

Pinball Machine

Do you ever feel like your grief is similar to a ball in a pinball machine, bouncing off bumpers, striving to maintain a high score? Some days, you will slip down and fall straight through the flippers at the bottom, hitting nothing along the way. Other days, you will get caught between bumpers that will drive you crazy as you flip from one emotion to the next. The aim of pinball is to score as high as possible without losing your balls; the goal in addressing your grief should be to maintain positive momentum without hitting too many emotional bumpers.

Day 347

Five Senses

Each of the five senses associated with the human body are touched by grief in different ways. While we can no longer directly hear, see, touch, smell, or taste our loved ones who have passed, we can connect with them via our senses.

Hearing the voice of your loved one through video recordings provides music to your ears with the special sound that will always remind you of him or her.

Seeing pictures of your loved one will provide a constant reminder of the beauty the person posses.

Touching your loved one's belongings will offer you warmth through objects that are associated with who he or she was.

Smelling his or her clothing or cologne/perfume provides a feeling of nostalgia and closeness—a special feeling that triggers great emotion.

Tasting the loved one's favorite foods will remind you of days of cooking, eating, and spending time together.

Day 348
Healthy Lifestyles

Maintain the newfound healthy lifestyle that you have created over the last year. Keep up the motivation, eat three meals a day, and exercise on a daily basis. Be sure to spend time relaxing and engaging with friends and family while working or going to school. Get up each day, dress as if you own the world, keep your shoulders back, and smile.

Day 349

Creating a Happy Home

With all the ups and downs you have experienced over the year, it is time to create a happy home. Make your house have life again; therefore it is time to:

- Cook regularly.
- Arrange fresh flowers.
- Play music.
- Entertain friends and family.
- Plan a holiday gathering.
- Spruce up areas that look tired.
- Paint a room.

Day 350
Flowers

There is something about flowers that can make anyone feel good. The vibrant colors, the beautiful shapes, and the wonderful fragrances bring life to any room or garden. Whether the flowers are part of a plant or remain on their stems in a vase, they have a tendency to enrich our lives through natural beauty.

Surround yourself with the gifts of flowers.

Day 351

Your New Journey

Year two starts the next phase of your grief with a new journey. All the grieving tools and guidance you have received from reading, friends, counselors, and family members during the first year of grief can be applied to set up the next path of your journey.

Your journey for year two should emphasize learning to live with the loss on a daily basis. Learning to reclaim your emotions, your home, your day, your social life, and your work obligations will help you with the next phase.

Create a plan, follow a path, and make your journey meaningful for you and your family.

Day 352
Courage

Working through grief takes courage. Knowing how to deal with the pain associated with the loss, fear in discovery of what is next in life, intimidation about having the strength to continue on, and the uncertainty of your future, all challenge your bravery.

Since the worst has already occurred, finding the guts to overcome your fear, pain, uncertainty, and intimidation will allow you to prove to yourself that you have the courage to persevere through your grief.

Day 353
Common Sense

Where does our common sense go when we are grieving?

Common sense is defined in *Merriam-Webster*'s dictionary as "sound and prudent judgment based on a simple perception of a situation or facts." Grieving the loss of a loved one clouds our judgment and often changes our perception, causing us to make decisions that might be irrational—yet we seem to carry on even if we make a few mistakes along the way.

As you approach the end of your first year of loss and continue to gain strength, you will find your common sense again, including the practical knowledge and judgment that is needed to help live a sensible and rational life.

Day 354

All That Truly Matters in the End Was You Were Loved

A comforting feeling to know the pain you endure during grief is in direct correlation to the love you shared with the person you lost. Whether the death was untimely or took its natural progression, knowing that you shared a loving bond with the person you lost is what you can cherish the rest of your life.

Day 355

Take Pleasure in Today

Enjoy today—don't think about yesterday or tomorrow. Find joy, gratification, and happiness in knowing that today is special.

Day 356
Ride a Bike

How many times have we heard the expression, "It's just like learning how to ride a bike," referring to the fact that once you acquire the skills, you have the ability the rest of your life.

As a kid, taking off your training wheels and learning how to ride a two-wheeler was so difficult, but once you got the hang of it there was no turning back. If working through grief was only that easy. In your grief journey you have acquired the skills needed to redefine your relationship with your loved one, learned how to manage your emotions, and embraced how important friends and family are to you. Take those newly found skills and get back on your bike, as they will provide the balance you need.

Day 357
Plan a Vacation

Whether it is a break from work, a break from the kids, a break from your grief, or a much-needed trip to get away from your routine, it is time to plan something fun and exciting.

Take into consideration your budget, climate choice, desired activities, and travel companion. Start researching and planning. Save the date. Pack the suitcase. Enjoy!

Day 358

Trailblazer

Trailblazers are known as people who "blaze" their way through life as they approach new and uncharted territory. Think of the settlers who moved west—what could they have possibly thought when they reached the Rocky Mountains, as they stood there in awe of their beauty, while also wondering how they would get up and over the mountains?

Your loss is a major hurdle that you will climb over, gaining strength from all aspects of your life. Be your own trailblazer.

Day 359
The Pain Subsides

While the pain may subside over time, you will always miss the presence of your loved one in your life—desiring to share new experiences, watching the person grow old with you, and, most of all, feeling the love.

Day 360
Maintain Your Community

You have spent the last year building a community of support around you. You have maintained and rebuilt relationships with family and friends, while developing new connections with people who are walking a similar journey. Keep your community close, rely on them for a variety of needs, and provide support to them when they need it.

Maintain your community.

Day 361
Create Your Own Strategic Plan

Usually found in a business setting, a strategic plan is a process for defining direction and making decisions. The plan is used to communicate the outlook of where the company would like to be in three to five years.

What about using the concept for your personal life?

Start with creating a vision of where you want to be. Then develop your mission, which clarifies how you will achieve your vision. When those are complete, define your values, which drive your priorities and framework for making decisions. Next you will create your strategy— often referred to as a roadmap—outlining the path to reach your goals.

Your strategic plan will evolve over time and often change. The concept is to come up with the plan and incorporate it into your daily life.

Day 362

Family and Friends

Your family and friends have been present in your life for the last year, wiping your tears, holding your hand, and supporting you the best they know how. At times you might have felt they offered advice when you needed it, and at other times they just could not understand the magnitude of your grief. Bottom line, they were there for you.

Always remember to:

- Cherish their love and support.
- Appreciate all they have done and continue to do.
- Be patient when they don't understand.
- Value their commitment to you.
- Help them when they need help.

Day 363

Keep Your Glass Half-Full

This phrase refers to optimism—half-full—or pessimism—half-empty—illustrating a point of view. Although the expression is philosophical in nature, it does provide a griever with the opportunity to consider looking at the challenges in life in a more positive manner.

Day 364

It's All about You

The challenge is putting you first—before family needs, before responsibilities, before work, before household chores, before volunteer commitments.

To successfully grieve the loss of a loved one, at some point you have to become the focal point. By now, the loss has shaped you and realigned your priorities, while time has helped fill the void caused by the absence. From now on, you are the most important piece of the equation. If you feel self-assured, all aspects of your life will fall into place.

It is all about you—so start with you first.

Day 365
Gone but Not Forgotten

Our loved ones are physically gone, but they will be with us forever. Their memories will be imprinted in our hearts forever, and we will share their love for eternity. Cherish that they entered our lives and that we were able to experience their love.

About the Author

As a motivational speaker, author, grief consultant, and facilitator, Rachel Blythe Kodanaz tackles today's challenges to help provide encouragement to those who are suffering a loss or setback. She entered the grief world in 1992 when her husband suddenly passed away, leaving her with a two-year-old daughter. Her experience in the management of large corporations led her to develop and publish material about how to support grief and loss in the workplace.

Rachel is a columnist for *Living with Loss Magazine* and has published numerous articles and handbooks on grief. She speaks nationally to various groups and has appeared on Good Morning America. Her passion drives her to help other grievers who are suffering losses by actively supporting national grief and loss programs, including Camp Widow, Facing the Mourning®, employee assistance programs, and human resource endeavors.

Visit Rachel online at www.rachelkodanaz.com.

"This book is the best gift you can give to yourself or someone else who is grieving."

—Jennifer McBride, President, HeartLight Center

"Written by a grief expert with a lot of talent, Rachel knows what she's talking about. This book can be opened to any page and compassionate comfort will be found."

—Andrea Gambill, Editor-in-Chief, *Grief Digest* magazine

"This book is filled with hope, practical advice, and a wisdom that will be helpful for those facing grief. I highly recommend it."

—Deborah Gauchat, PhD, Licensed Psychologist

Living with Loss, One Day at a Time offers daily encouragement to individuals and families who have recently lost a loved one. By providing tools and suggestions that offer hope, optimism, introspection, and self-discovery, this accessible and comforting guide enables readers to embrace the happy and healthy days of life with their loved one while integrating and accepting their loss into everyday life.

As a motivational speaker, author, grief consultant, and facilitator, **Rachel Blythe Kodanaz** provides encouragement to those who are suffering a loss. Rachel is a columnist for *Living with Loss Magazine* and has appeared on *Good Morning America*.

$15.95 US   Self Help | Death, Grief, Bereavement

ISBN: 978-1-938486-31-9

5 1 5 9 5

9 781938 486319

A Fulcrum Paperback Original
www.fulcrumbooks.com

FULCRUM PUBLISHING